101	水	121	往						
102	氷	122	注						
103	永	123	駐	143	形	163	細	183	官
104	馬	124	駅	144	型	164	畑	184	管
105	鳥	125	訳	145	親	165	旅	185	市
106	島	126	快	146	新	166	族	186	布
107	可	127	決	147	近	167	組	187	都
108	何	128	央	148	所	168	祖	188	部
109	河	129	英	149	道	169	福	189	郡
110	向	130	歩	150	通	170	副	190	群
111	同	131	走	151	週	171	祭	191	庭
112	荷	132	足	152	追	172	察	192	席
113	付	133	車	153	迫	173	店	193	座
114	府	134	事	154	泊	174	屋	194	度
115	符	135	書	155	券	175	室	195	原
116	王	136	列	156	巻	176	堂	196	源
117	玉	137	例	157	田	177	空	197	料
118	宝	138	幹	158	由	178	究	198	科
119	主	139	輸	159	曲	179	家	199	老
120	住	140	輪	160	申	180	安	200	考

Kanji Connections

Hints on How to Differentiate 400 Easily Confused Characters

Tae Moriyama

Translated by Bob and Reiko Gavey

SHUFUNOTOMO CO., LTD.

Other Tae Moriyama books published by Shufunotomo

•

Weekend Adventures Outside Tokyo
Tokyo Adventures

Book design by Toshiaki Suzuki
Cover illustration by Kohei Ohno
Kanji illustrations by Yasuo Fukuda

First Printing, 1998

Published by SHUFUNOTOMO CO., LTD.
2-9 Kanda Surugadai, Chiyoda-ku, Tokyo 101-8911, Japan

ISBN 4-07-976592-4

Printed in Japan

TABLE OF CONTENTS

INTRODUCTION

While teaching Japanese language classes over the years I have found that foreign students tend to make certain common mistakes, either confusing similar-looking kanji with each other, or mixing up antonyms which share the same radical.

For example, students frequently confuse [休] (rest, vacation) with [体] (body), or misidentify [閉] and [開] as "open" and "close," respectively, when actually the meanings are the other way around. To help them differentiate between [休] and [体], say, I might mention that the former is a combination of [亻] (person) and [木] (tree). In olden times, when farming was the predominant occupation, a person would normally relax in the shade of a nearby tree when tired, which explains why this kanji has meanings associated with taking a rest. The character [体], on the other hand, combines [亻] (person) and [本] (something of importance, or the root of something). And the thing that is most important as the "root" of a person is, of course, the body. In this way I give my students hints to help them remember the differences between kanji that are similar in appearance. This book is a compilation of these hints.

You may think that Japanese people would be beyond such confusion, but actually this is a struggle that everybody has to face. I found myself in the same predicament when writing this book, when I discovered that I was not so confident about some characters after all, and had to check them in the dictionary. One thing is certain: anything that is left unclear will remain in doubt forever. Well begun is half done, as the saying goes, which is why it is important to begin in the right way, firmly imprinting the different features of each kanji on one's mind at an early stage.
From its inception, the main aim of this book was to clarify, as much as possible, the differences between similar-looking kanji based on their etymological roots. But when I began writing I was immediately

confronted by two major obstacles. First, many kanji were greatly simplified in the years following World War II, and it is now sometimes impossible to imagine their roots from their current form. I realized that the only way to treat such kanji was to find some kind of expedient as a memory aid.

One example of this is the description given for *hidari* [左], meaning "left." There is no problem with the associated kanji, *migi* [右] (right), which consists of [ナ] (hand) and [口] (mouth), because the meaning here, using the right hand to carry food to the mouth, is readily apparent. But the roots of *hidari*, in which hand [ナ] is combined with [工], representing a traditional ruler or scale used for construction work (which would normally be held in the left hand), are not so helpful because this type of tool is rarely seen today. While I was puzzling over how to handle this kanji, one of my foreign friends pointed out that, if turned on its side, it looked somewhat like the roman letter *H*, reminding her of *hidari*. I have incorporated this excellent suggestion into the description for that kanji, and am happy to report that the book has benefited greatly from international collaboration such as this. Even if these expedients are a little far-fetched at times, I have used them as long as they offer the reader an interesting and easy-to-remember clue to the meaning of a kanji.

The second obstacle that confronted me was that not just one but several different etymological roots are often attributed to a given kanji. In fact, it sometimes seems that there are the same number of theories for the roots of a particular kanji as there are reference materials by experts in this field. In such cases, I decided to use the theory that would be the easiest for the reader to understand and assimilate as a memory aid. I mentioned earlier that it is important to begin in the right way and, following this approach, I have described the simpler characters first so that the reader can clearly distinguish them from the start. The 400 easily confused kanji included here are among those that are used the most frequently, and were selected with the aim of assisting the reader on a practical, day-to-day basis. To help readers visualize the roots of various characters, illustrations are also included where appropriate. As a reference, a list of radicals that appear in the book is given at the beginning, as well as a note on the readings of kanji. And exercises are included at the end so that readers can test their knowledge after studying the text. These exercises are quite simple, and are not intended to be arduous or exhaustive, so I hope you will attempt them in a playful spirit.

This brings me to the title of the book, *Kanji Connections*, which not only denotes the connections between two or more similar kanji, but also has the added nuance of building connections between the student of Japanese and the kanji that must be learned in order to master the language. Remember that kanji are difficult for everyone! But they are also deeply fascinating, with their subtle shades of meaning, the stories associated with them, and the philosophies they embody. My sincere hope in writing this book is that it will bring the world of kanji closer to you and help you to become familiar with it.

It is often said that life is a series of small connections and coincidences, and the process by which this book came into being was no exception to this. One day I was asked by a student whether bookstores carried any reference works that grouped similar-looking characters together. Since Japanese people also have problems in this regard I was sure that something along these lines must be available. But on checking various stores I found that nothing quite like this had been published. The only solution was to write such a book myself, and that was how it all began. The student who first asked me this question was Eloise Pearson Hamatani, and I would like to offer my sincere appreciation to her for the wealth of valuable suggestions she has given me since then, including which kanji to select for inclusion.

I would also like to thank the staff of the International Department of Shufunotomo Co., Ltd., particularly Shunichi Kamiya, general manager, for surmounting the difficulties inherent in preparing a book like this and creating such a beautiful publication. Kamiya-san asked me to write a book dealing with the Japanese language some time ago, and it is with a sense of relief that I have at last completed this task. Thanks should also go to Kate Gorringe-Smith and Yumi Nakada, who edited and formatted the text, for their efforts during the long process of readying this book for publication.

Finally, I would like to express my sincere gratitude to Bob and Reiko Gavey for their work translating all of the manuscripts, while at the same time offering advice on the explanations and even conceiving the title. Their assistance at each stage of preparing the book is greatly appreciated.

Tae Moriyama
September, 1998

A NOTE ON THE READINGS OF KANJI

There are many theories regarding when kanji (Chinese characters) were introduced into Japan from China and, although nobody is certain, it is likely that this took place around the second or third century A.D. Two types of readings evolved for these imported characters: (1) *on* (or *on-yomi*), the Chinese phonetical readings, which approximated the pronunciations of the characters in China at that time; and (2) *kun* (or *kun-yomi*), the Japanese readings, in which a word that had been used in Japan since olden times was assigned to a particular kanji. Some kanji have only *on-yomi* or only *kun-yomi*, while others have several of either or both types of readings. These variations arose due to differences in the time of introduction or the importation of the same kanji from different regions in China.

For each kanji in this book, the *on-yomi* are written first in katakana followed by the *kun-yomi* in hiragana. As an example, the readings of [日] are divided into the *on-yomi* [ニチ] and [ジツ], and the *kun-yomi* [ひ] and [か], while those for [花] are [カ] and [はな], respectively. The *on-yomi* is convenient for forming phrases through combinations with other kanji, but if pronounced by itself (such as *ka* [カ]), the meaning will not be understood because there are many kanji with the same pronunciation. In the case of the *kun-yomi*, however, the meaning of the kanji concerned is generally clear even when it is read in isolation (such as *hana* [はな]).

A few words about hiragana and katakana may be useful here. Kanji are ideograms rather than phonetic elements, with each character having an inherent meaning, so a system of phonograms was necessary in order to master their readings. The two syllabaries, hiragana and katakana, were therefore developed in Japan about 1,100 years ago, in the early part of the Heian era (794 - 1185), using kanji as a base. Hiragana was created by remodeling whole kanji characters into a soft and simplified cursive style, and was mainly used by women — who did not study the Chinese classics — for writing letters and poetry. (An example is the hiragana character *a* [あ], which is a modification of the kanji [安].) Katakana, on the other hand, was created by taking individual elements of kanji as separate units and giving them a hard or angular shape. (For example, the katakana character *e* [エ], which originally formed a part of [江].) Katakana was employed for particles and verb conjugations in studies where Chinese classical literature was rendered in Japanese phonetical form.

Today, katakana is used mainly for words of foreign origin, while everyday text appearing in newspapers, magazines and books is generally a combination of kanji and hiragana, since this is easier to read.

In the past, Chinese dictionaries contained about 50,000 kanji. Both China and Japan have moved toward the simplification of kanji over the years, however, and the Japanese Ministry of Education currently defines 1,945 characters as *jōyō kanji* (kanji designated for daily use) to be mastered during the nine years of cumpulsory education. Among these, the kanji used most frequently on a practical basis — 1,006 in total — are designated as kanji to be studied during the six years of elementary school education. The 400 kanji in this book have thus mainly been selected from these 1,006 characters.

RADICALS MENTIONED IN THIS BOOK

(in the order that they appear)

■ *HEN*
(the left-hand element of kanji that can be divided into left and right parts)

亻	*ninben*: person
日	*hihen*: sun, day
扌	*tehen*: hand
彳	*gyōninben*: travel along a path or road
牛	*ushihen*: cow or bull
礻	*shimesuhen*: god or deity
氵	*sanzui*: water
木	*kihen*: tree
土	*tsuchihen*: soil or ground
馬	*umahen*: horse
言	*gonben*: words or speaking
忄	*risshinben*: heart, in a spiritual or emotional sense
車	*kurumahen*: wheel or vehicle
阝	*kozatohen*: hill or mound formed by piles of earth
糸	*itohen*: thread
米	*komehen*: rice
禾	*nogihen*: ear of rice or some other cereal
金	*kanehen*: metal
女	*onnahen*: woman
弓	*yumihen*: bow (for shooting arrows)
王	*ōhen*: king
食	*shokuhen*: food, to eat
耳	*mimihen*: ear
目	*mehen*: eyes
口	*kuchihen*: mouth
月	*nikuzuki* or *tsukihen*: This radical is normally called *nikuzuki* in words that are associated with parts of the body, and *tsukihen* in other contexts.
衤	*koromohen*: clothes
石	*ishihen*: stone
貝	*kaihen*: shell, money

■ *TSUKURI*
(the right-hand element of kanji that can be divided into left and right parts)

力	*chikara*: force or power
刂	*rittō*: sword
阝	*ōzato*: enclosure of a village or town
殳	*rumata*: halberd (a type of lance) being held in the hand and, by extension, the use of a tool
攵	*nobun*: stick or rod held in the hand
頁	*ōgai*: head

■ *KANMURI*
(the upper element of kanji that can be divided into upper and lower parts)

宀	*ukanmuri*: roof of a house
艹	*kusakanmuri*: grass, plant
竹	*takekanmuri*: bamboo
穴	*anakanmuri*: hole
雨	*amekanmuri*: rain

■ *ASHI*
(the lower element of kanji that can be divided into upper and lower parts)

貝	*kai*: money, an expression for counting
皿	*sara*: container
心	*kokoro*: heart, in a spiritual or emotional sense

■ *KAMAE*
(an enclosing type element)

門	*mongamae*: gate
囗	*kunigamae*: enclosure
戈	*hokogamae*: halberd (a type of lance)
行	*gyōgamae*: to go or come
弋	*shikigamae*: sign or mark

■ *TARE*
(an element extending from the upper part of a kanji to the lower left)

广	*madare*: building
厂	*gandare*: cliff

■ *NYŌ*
(an element shaped like a combination of *hen* and *ashi*)

辶	*shinnyō*: to travel along a path or road, or advance
廴	*ennyō*: to extend or advance

KANJI CONNECTIONS

1

日

■[ニチ, ジツ; ひ] day, sun; [か] suffix for counting days

■ This kanji was derived from the shape of the sun. There are many words with meanings related to the sun or to days that contain this character as a radical.

■[日曜日(にちようび)] Sunday; [三日(みっか)] 3 days; 3rd of the month

2

白

■[ハク, ビャク; しろ, しろ(い), しら] white

■ The rays of the sun [日], although colorless in reality, have traditionally been considered to be white by the Japanese. The small stroke at the top left of this character signifies such a ray and, by extension, white.

■[白鳥(はくちょう)] white swan

3

百

■[ヒャク] hundred

■ A novel way to remember this kanji is to visualize it lying on its side: [|Ⅲ] →100.

■[百円(ひゃくえん)] 100 yen

4

■[モク, ボク, め, ま] eye; [め] ordinal suffix

■This kanji is modeled after the shape of an eye. It is also used as a suffix to indicate ordinal numbers in expressions of sequence, order, and so on (1st, 2nd, 3rd, etc.).

■[目的(もくてき)]purpose;[三番目(さんばんめ)]the third

5

■[ジ, シ] self; [みずか(ら)] in person

■Believe it or not, this kanji was derived from the shape of the human nose. A good way to distinguish it from *me* [目] is to think of the stroke at the top left as a finger pointing to a nose, remembering that the Japanese traditionally point to their nose when referring to themselves. Hence its meaning: self.

■[自分(じぶん)]oneself

6

■[シュ; くび] neck, head

■Here we have a combination that expresses the concept of neck and head through the addition of hair [䒑] on top of [自], the character based on the shape of a nose. Which is quite logical, when you think about it a little. (See also Nos. 363 and 364.)

■[首都(しゅと)]capital (city), metropolis

■[ケン; み(る)] to see, look; [み(える)] to be seen, visible; [み(せる)] to show

■ This kanji consists of an eye [目] supported by a pair of legs [儿], denoting the concept of vision. To avoid confusing this kanji with the next one, *kai* [貝] (shellfish), remember that *mi(ru)* has the longer legs.

■[見物 (けんぶつ)] sightseeing

8

■[かい] shellfish; shell

■ The upper part of this kanji was derived from the shape of a shellfish rather than an eye. And as we all know, if a shellfish has any leg-like protuberances, they are undeniably short. In ancient times, shells were used as currency, so this character appears as the radical *kai* in a number of kanji related to money.

■[貝類 (かいるい)] shellfish

9

■[イン] member

■ The combination of *kuchi* [口] (mouth) above and *kai* [貝] below originally indicated circular currency, or coins. Later on it evolved into an expression for counting, and finally became a word used to count or identify people.

■[会社員 (かいしゃいん)] company employee

10

■[バイ; か(う)] to buy, purchase

■ This kanji looks very similar to the last one, but here the upper part represents a net. Just as birds and fish were traditionally caught with nets, other daily necessities were obtained by paying money (shells). Hence its meaning: to buy.

■[買(か)い物(もの)] shopping

11

■[バイ; う(る)] sale; to sell; [う(れる)] to be saleable, in demand

■ And while we're on the subject of buying things, let's look at the kanji with the opposite meaning: to sell. This kanji originated from a combination of two characters: [士] (to come out or put out) and [買] (to buy). If one puts out on display something one has purchased, one wishes to sell it.

■[売店(ばいてん)] kiosk

12

■[ショウ; ちい(さい), こ, お] small, minor

■ Originally, this kanji consisted of three small dots (see diagram) to express something small. As time went on it evolved into three vertical strokes and finally to the present-day [小], but retained its original meaning.

■[小学校(しょうがっこう)] elementary school

13

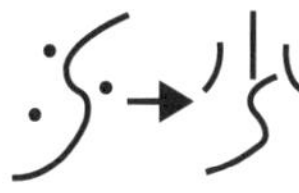

■[ショウ; すく(ない), すこ(し)] few, little

■ Here we see the character [小] with an additional diagonal line. This kanji began as the symbol shown on the left in the diagram, developed into the right hand character, then finally became [少]. The extra diagonal line signifies that if a small object, or group of objects, is divided into two parts, one will be left with even smaller portions.

■[少々(しょうしょう)] a few, a small amount

14

■[ダイ, タイ; おお, おお(きい)] large, great; [おお(いに)] greatly, very much

■ This kanji represents a person with arms and legs outstretched, indicating large and, by extension, great.

■[大学(だいがく)] university; [大雨(おおあめ)] heavy rain

15

■[テン; あめ, あま] sky, heaven

■ By adding a line above the person depicted in the character *dai* [大], we get the kanji for the sky, stretching overhead.

■[天気(てんき)] weather

16

■[ゲン, ガン; もと] beginning, foundation, origin

■ This kanji represents the shape of a person, with the two lines at the top denoting the head. The concept conveyed here is that our head is where our thoughts originate.

■[元気(げんき)] vigor, energy, vitality

17

■[タイ, タ; ふと(い)] large, fat, thick;
[ふと(る)] to become fat

■ This kanji signifies 'large on top of large' [大大], with the small stroke in the lower part serving as an abbreviation of the second character, instead of having to write the same character twice. This conveys the concept of being large, fat or thick.

■[太平洋(たいへいよう)] Pacific Ocean

18

■[ケン; いぬ] dog

■ This kanji is actually derived from the shape of a dog. An easy way to remember it is to think of the small stroke at the upper right as one of its ears.

■[小犬(こいぬ)] small dog, puppy

19

■[ジョウ, ショウ; うえ] top, on, upper; [うわ, かみ] upper part; [あ(げる)] to raise; [あ(がる), の(ぼる)] to rise, go up

■When Chinese characters were first being devised, words for abstract concepts that could not be modeled on a particular physical shape were expressed by symbols. An example of this was the symbol shown in the diagram on the left, which consists of a round mark or dot drawn above a horizontal line, and signifies the idea of top or upper. This was later modified by the addition of a vertical line to give the present-day kanji [上].

■[上手(じょうず)] skill, proficiency; [上着(うわぎ)] jacket

20

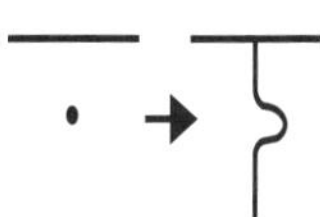

■[カ, ゲ; した, しも, もと] bottom, under, lower; base; [さ(げる)] to hang (something), to lower; [さ (がる)] to hang down; [くだ(る)] to go down; [くだ (す), お(ろす)] to lower, hand down; [くだ(さる)] to give; [お(りる)] to get off (a vehicle), get down

■In the opposite way to [上], this kanji began as a round mark or dot drawn below a horizontal line, signifying bottom or lower. The subsequent addition of a vertical line produced the kanji [下].

■[下水(げすい)] sewerage, drainage; [下着(したぎ)] underwear

21

■[ホウ] direction, side; [かた] direction; person; way (of doing)

■A good way to differentiate this kanji from its cousin, *man* [万], which follows next, is to think that the stroke at the top is pointing in a certain direction.

■[方面(ほうめん)] district; way; [方法(ほうほう)] method

22

■[マン] ten thousand; [バン] many, all

■This kanji is said to have originated from the Buddhist symbol *manji* [卍]. Although unrelated to the former meaning, it took the pronunciation *man* and is used to express a large number. It may be helpful here to think of a long sutra containing a large number of pages.

■[一万円(いちまんえん)] 10,000 yen

23

■[リョク, リキ; ちから] force, power, strength

■When one exerts one's strength, the muscles of the arm stand out like the stroke extending from the top of this kanji.

■[力士(りきし)] sumo wrestler

24

刀

■[トウ; かたな] sword, knife

■ This kanji was derived from the shape of a sword, and also means to cut off. As an aid to differentiating it from *chikara* [力] above, imagine that the top part has been cut off cleanly by a sword, so that there is no stroke protruding.

■[名刀(めいとう)] a fine sword

25

■[キュウ, ク; ここの, ここの(つ)] nine

■ This kanji originated from the shape of an arm with the muscles flexed and the hand forming a fist, a gesture which used to be associated with going to the end or the limit, or with mastering something. This, in turn, came to represent the highest numeral, 9.

■[九時(くじ)] nine o'clock

26

■[ガン; まる, まる(い)] round; [まる(める)] to form into a ball

■ Although similar to the preceding kanji, this kanji depicts a person curled around something important (represented here by [丶]). Hence its meaning: round or formed into a ball. You can differentiate this character from the preceding kanji by remembering that the slanting dash represents something important.

■[日の丸(ひのまる)] *Hi no maru* (the 'Rising Sun,' or Japanese flag)

27

■[ジン, ニン; ひと] person

■This character is modeled after the shape of a person standing. The radical *ninben* [亻], which is derived from it, is often seen in the left-hand position in words related to people or humanity, and is also expressed in the katakana character [イ], or *i*. As a memory aid, draw the katakana [イ] in the air with your finger; the kanji closest to that shape is [人].

■[外国人 (がいこくじん)] foreigner

28

■[ニュウ] entering; [い(る), はい(る)] to enter, get in; [い(れる)] to put in, let in

■The original form of this character signified an entrance (see diagram). Compared to the preceding kanji, the stroke on the left is shorter while that on the right is longer. A convenient way to memorize this kanji is to simply remember that it is the mirror image of [人].

■[入口 (いりぐち)] an entrance

29

■[キュウ] rest, vacation; [やす(む)] to rest; [やす(める)] to give (something) a rest; [やす(まる)] to be rested

■Now we come to a group of kanji with the left-hand radical *ninben* [亻], meaning person. In the first of these, the representation of a tree [木] is on the right. The connotation here is easy to spot: when it's time to take a break, a person working in the fields finds a shady tree under which to rest.

■[休憩 (きゅうけい)] rest, break; [休日 (きゅうじつ)] holiday, day off

30

■[タイ, テイ; からだ] body

■This time the character on the right is *hon* [本], meaning something of importance, or the root of something. And the root of a person is, of course, their body.

■[身体(しんたい)] the human body

31

■[シ] use; messenger; [つか(う)] to use

■This kanji also has *ninben* [亻] on the left, while [吏] (government official), is on the right. Government officials employ people to do various tasks, so this kanji means use. An easy way to distinguish it from *ben* [便], below, is to keep in mind two traits of such officials: they use their mouth [口] to order people around, and occupy a prominent position, like that of the vertical line [ナ] protruding from the top here.

■[大使館(たいしかん)] embassy

32

■[ベン] convenience; [ビン] mail

■Here, the element on the right [更] represents the concept of reforming or improving something that is inconvenient. In other words, people change the world around them to make things more convenient.

■[便利(べんり)] convenience; [郵便局(ゆうびんきょく)] post office

33

■[サク, サ; つく(る)] to make

■*Ninben* appears once again on the left, and on the right we see the shape of a half-built house. Combining these ideas, we have the notion of a person building or making something.

■[作品(さくひん)] product, piece of work

34

■[サク] yesterday, the past, ancient times

■The radical on the left this time is *hihen* [日] which symbolizes the sun, and also means day. On the right is the shape of a half-built house, as we saw in the preceding kanji. This combination denotes that which existed in the past, or yesterday.

■[昨日(さくじつ)] yesterday

35

■[シュ; て, た] hand

■This kanji is formed from the shape of the palm and the arm; the radical *tehen* [扌] is derived from the same root. Remember that the kanji *te* and the radical *tehen*, which both signify the hand, curve toward the left.

■[手紙(てがみ)] letter

36

毛

■[モウ; け] hair, wool; feather, down

■ Here we have a character modeled after the tail of an animal, this time stretching toward the right. This gives us the kanji for hair.

■[毛布 (もうふ)] woolen blanket; [毛糸 (けいと)] woolen yarn

37

■[ユウ, ウ; みぎ] right

■ Most people use their right hand to carry food to their mouth. This kanji is an easy one to remember, since it consists of [𠂇] signifying the hand, and [口] meaning *kuchi*, or mouth.

■[右手 (みぎて)] the right hand

38

■[サ; ひだり] left

■ This kanji also includes the representation of a hand [𠂇], but instead of a mouth, beneath it is the character [工], as seen in the word *kōji* [工事], or construction. This indicates a ruler or scale, a tool that would normally be held in the left hand. Another way to remember this kanji is to visualize it lying on its side [[illegible]]; the 'H' may jog your memory as to its meaning: *hidari*, or left.

■[左側 (ひだりがわ)] the left side

39

■[シ, ス; こ] child

■ This kanji was formed from the shape of an infant, and means child. If you use your imagination a little, you can picture the upper part as the head of the child, and the horizontal stroke as its outstretched arms.

■[親子（おやこ）] parent(s) and child(ren); [調子（ちょうし）] condition; way, manner; (in) tune, tone

40

■[ヨ] previously, in advance

■ This is one of those kanji whose roots are not very useful as a guide to the current meaning. But notice how the upper element is identical to the katakana character *ma* [マ]. And, if you use your imagination again, the lower element [了] also has similarities to an elongated *ma*. This coincidental association with the character *ma* can be a helpful device for remembering the meaning of this kanji—just think of the expression *mae-motte* [まえもって], meaning previously or in advance, or *mae kara* [まえから], meaning from before. (Note, however, that these two expressions are written with a different kanji, *mae* [前], and are merely given here as a memory aid.)

■[予定（よてい）] program, plan, schedule; [予約（よやく）] booking, reservation

41

■[ジ] mark, character, letter

■ The upper radical here, *ukanmuri* [宀], signifies the roof of a house, while the lower element [子] means child. Just as children grow up and make a home of their own in which to raise their family, kanji characters are born of other characters in a seemingly endless succession. Just ask any student of the Japanese language!

■[漢字(かんじ)] kanji

42

■[ガク] science, learning; [まな(ぶ)] to learn

■ This kanji was formerly much more complicated, with [字], representing a child in a building, in the lower position, surmounted by an element symbolizing the hands of a teacher linked together with those of a student. The concept conveyed by this rather top-heavy character of 17 strokes was, of course, children learning hand-in-hand with their teacher in a building. In the present-day character, the upper element has been simplified to [⺍] perhaps reflecting the fact that the bond between teacher and student has become weaker. On the other hand, the requirements of the educational curriculum have undoubtedly become heavier.

■[学生(がくせい)] student; [医学(いがく)] medical science, medicine

43

動

■[ドウ] movement; [うご(く)] to move; [うご(かす)] to move (something)

■ The left part of this kanji consists of [重], meaning heavy, while on the right is the radical *chikara* [力], meaning force or power. This signifies that when force is applied, even a heavy thing can be moved.

■[自動車(じどうしゃ)] automobile

44

働

■[ドウ] work; [はたら(く)] to work

■ On the left is the familiar radical *ninben* [亻], meaning person, while the remaining part of this kanji is the character [動], meaning to move. Work almost always entails moving the body — it's hard to achieve anything whilst sitting perfectly still.

■[労働者(ろうどうしゃ)] laborer

45

■[ジ] durability; [も(つ)] to have, hold, possess; to maintain

■ The left-hand radical here is *tehen* [扌], which represents using the hand. Think of holding something in your hand for a long time, as an aid to remembering both meanings of this kanji and distinguishing it from the next character, *ma(tsu)*.

■[金持(かねも)ち] wealthy person

46

■[タイ; ま(つ)] to wait (for)

■The radical on the left here is *gyōninben* [彳], signifying travel along a path or road, and on the right is the character for temple [寺]. The original components of this right-hand character signified work performed through the movement of arms and legs; this evolved into the concept of a public office where people gathered and worked, and finally into a temple as a place where priests were accommodated. Since the concept of waiting is not readily apparent from the combination of elements in this kanji, a convenient way to remember its meaning might be to think of *gyōninben* as meaning two people, leading to the image of someone waiting for someone else in the grounds of a temple.

■[待合室(まちあいしつ)] waiting room

47

時

■[ジ; とき] time, hour

■The next member of this group has the radical *hihen* [日], representing the sun, on the left. As explained in No. 46, the right-hand character [寺], meaning temple, was derived from original components that signified work performed through the movement of arms and legs. As the sun 'works,' time passes, indicating the core meaning: a length of time. And, as an additional aid, keep in mind that in bygone years people knew what time it was due to the striking of a bell in their local temple.

■[時刻(じこく)] the hour, the time; [同時通訳(どうじつうやく)] simultaneous interpreting

48 特

■[トク] special

■On the left here is the radical *ushihen* [牜] (see No. 90), meaning cow or bull, and again the character for temple is on the right. So how does the concept of a temple relate to *ushihen*? Well, keep in mind the core meaning, work, that is associated with the character for temple. Cattle are special because they are traditionally the best workers among all domestic animals, so this kanji came to mean special.

■[特急(とっきゅう)] limited/special express (train)

49 物

■[ブツ, モツ; もの] thing, article

■In this kanji, the character [勿] on the right means thing. And what better way to represent the definitive 'thing' among all things, than to combine this character with *ushihen* [牜] on the left, signifying the cow or bull, the most valuable of all livestock.

■[動物(どうぶつ)] animal

50 土

■[ド, ト;つち] ground, earth, soil

■Now we come to a pair of kanji that are easily confused. The first of these, *tsuchi*, represents a tree or other type of plant sprouting from the soil. The base, which signifies the surface of the earth, is naturally the longest line.

■[土地(とち)] land

51

士

■[シ] scholar, man, samurai

■The second member of this pair is formed from a combination of the numbers 1 [一] and 10 [十]. A good way to remember it is to think of the lower line as representing 1, so of course it is the shorter. This kanji denotes a specialist, or a person who has a deep knowledge of something—from '1 to 10' (or A to Z). It is also sometimes used simply to mean man.

■[弁護士(べんごし)] lawyer; [武士(ぶし)] samurai

52

社

■[シャ] company; shrine; [やしろ] shrine

■The radical on the left here, *shimesuhen* [礻], is based on the shape of an altar and signifies a god or deity. The right-hand part represents the earth. In the days when life revolved around farming this kanji came to depict, in the form of a shrine, the connection between a deity and the land. Most communities back then centered around a shrine, giving a clue to the root of words that are associated with society.

■[社会(しゃかい)] society, community; [神社(じんじゃ)] Shinto shrine

53

仕

■[シ, ジ] work; [つか(える)] to serve

■The left-hand radical this time is *ninben* [亻], which means person in a general sense, while—as we have just seen—the right-hand character *shi* [士] more specifically refers to a person of high position. This kanji conveys the concept of a person being near to someone in a higher position or, in other words, serving or working for that person.

■[仕事(しごと)] work, job

54

■[ボ; はは] mother

■ The kanji for mother is formed by adding two small dashes [⺀], signifying the breasts, to a slightly modified version of the character for woman [女], thus expressing the idea of a mother nurturing a child with milk. Note that in the following three kanji, the two small dashes are replaced by a single vertical stroke to form the element [毋].

ぼこくご
■[母国語] one's mother tongue

55

■[マイ] every, each

■ Here we have a mother depicted with an ornamental hairpin in her hair. Just as a mother traditionally gave birth to a swift succession of children (in the old days, at any rate), this kanji indicates something repetitive or successively increasing.

まいにち
■[毎日] every day

56

■[カイ; うみ] sea, ocean

■ The combination of the radical *sanzui* [氵], meaning water, and the character [毎] derived from the original concept of mother, signifies the ocean as the mother of everything on earth. Take care not to confuse *umi* [海] with the similar-sounding word *ume* [梅] described next.

かいがん
■[海岸] seashore, coast

57

■[バイ; うめ] Japanese apricot (fruit or tree), often referred to as 'Japanese plum'

■ With the radical *kihen* [木], meaning tree, on the left, and the derivation from mother again on the right, we have the kanji for the *ume*, or Japanese apricot, which is known for the large number of fruit it produces.

■[[梅干し(うめぼし)] pickled Japanese apricots, 'salted plums'

58

■[ユウ; とも] friend

■ This kanji is formed from the shape of two people clasping each other's hands: one hand is represented by [𠂇], and the other by [又]. This action probably indicates that they are friends.

■[友達(ともだち)] friend(s)

59

■[ハン, ホン] anti-; [そ(る), そ(らす)] to warp, bend back

■ In contrast to the preceding kanji, this one signifies a hand [又] pressing a thin board [厂] so as to warp it. If the pressure is released, the board returns to its normal shape, so this kanji also means going back or returning.

■[反対(はんたい)] opposition, objection; the opposite

60

■[フ; ちち] father

■ This kanji originated from the shape of a hand holding an axe, expressing the idea of a father as head of the household going out to hunt animals.

■[父親（ちちおや）] father

61

■[コウ; まじ(わる), まじ(える), ま(ぜる), ま(じる), ま(ざる), か(う), か(わす)] to mix/be mixed, to associate with, to exchange

■ The shape of this kanji is based on that of a person with crossed legs, which conveys the concept of converging or associating with others.

■[交番（こうばん）] police box

62

■[ブン,モン; ふみ] writings, sentence

■ Here we have a character that originated in the crisscross patterns that were traditionally used to decorate earthenware. From this arose a variety of connotations, including pattern, character, sentence, study, and similar concepts.

■[文学（ぶんがく）] literature

63

地

■[チ, ジ] earth, land

■This kanji has the radical *tsuchihen* [扌], which signifies the ground, on the left, while the right-hand part [也] represents a snake. Taken together, these elements symbolize the natural undulations of hills and valleys, reminiscent of the form of a snake.

ち か てつ
■[地下鉄] subway

64

他

■[タ; ほか] other, another

■Here we see *ninben* [亻], a person, on the left, combined with the representation of a snake on the right. The snake, being a disagreeable creature as far as most people are concerned, represents a person with whom one would rather not associate. Hence this kanji means otherness or a stranger.

た にん
■[他人] other people, stranger(s)

65

池

■[チ; いけ] pond

■The left-hand radical here is *sanzui* [氵], signifying water, and again on the right we find a snake. To remember this kanji, it might help to think of a pond with a curved shape like that of a snake.

いけぶくろ
■[池袋] Ikebukuro (district of Tokyo)

66

■[トウ; ひがし] east

■ This is an easy character to remember. It is formed from the sun [日] seen through the branches of a tree [木], and therefore signifies east, as this is the direction in which the sun rises.

■[東北(とうほく)] northeast, the Tōhoku region

67

■[ソク; たば] suffix for counting bundles; bunch

■ After collecting a load of wood [木] for the fire, one would normally tie it in a bundle. And that is what is represented by this kanji, which therefore signifies something that has been bundled together.

■[花束(はなたば)] a bouquet of flowers; [約束(やくそく)] a promise

68

■[セイ, サイ; にし] west

■ This kanji takes its form from the shape of a bird perching on its nest. Birds return to their nests as dusk approaches; hence its meaning: west, the direction in which the sun sets.

■[西洋(せいよう)] the West, Western countries

69

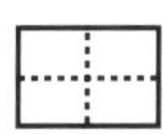

■[シ; よ, よ(つ), よっ(つ), よん] four

■ Here we have a square [口] containing two strokes [丷] which signify division. If a square is divided in two, both vertically and horizontally, four identical smaller squares are created. Thus the concept of four is expressed.

■[四角(しかく)] a square

70

■[リョウ] two, both

■ This kanji is in the shape of a set of scales, and is used in words that represent two things that form a set, like the balanced left and right sides of the scales.

■[両方(りょうほう)] both

71

■[ウ; あめ, あま] rain

■ Although this kanji looks similar, the concept that is depicted here is raindrops [⁚⁚] falling from inside a cloud.

■[大雨(おおあめ)] heavy rain, downpour; [風雨(ふうう)] wind and rain, rainstorm

72

■[エン] yen; circle; [まる(い)] round

■The original form of this familiar kanji included the character for shellfish or shell [貝] (see No. 8), giving the meaning currency or money. Money circulates from person to person, so this symbol also became associated with things that are circular or round.

■[五百円(ごひゃくえん)] 500 yen

73

■[ヨウ] business; usage; [もち(いる)] to use

■Here we have a kanji derived from the shape of a nail driven through a rectangular piece of wood. Nails are used to make various things; hence the meaning to use and, by extension, business.

■[用事(ようじ)] business, engagement; [利用(りよう)] utilization, use

74

■[サツ, サク] a volume, a copy

■In contrast to the preceding kanji, here we have two vertical strokes and one longer horizontal line. Once, before paper was developed, pieces of wood or bamboo were shaved into thin strips and bound with twine to make books. This kanji is modeled after such a book. From these roots it became a word for counting copies or volumes of books and magazines.

■[五冊(ごさつ)] five copies (of a book or magazine)

75

光

■[コウ; ひかり] light; [ひか(る)] to shine, be luminous

■ Now we come to a kanji with [⺌] on top, which is a modification of the character *hi* [火], denoting fire or flame, while the base represents the legs of a person [儿]. This combination signifies a person holding a burning torch, so means to shine, as well as meaning light itself.

■[光線(こうせん)] a beam of light; [日光(にっこう)] sunlight

76

先

■[セン; さき] previous, ahead

■ The upper part [⺧] of this kanji symbolizes a sprout or new leaf of grass growing upward. This is, again, placed on a base that represents legs. From this combination comes the idea of a person progressing or advancing, which in turn leads to the meaning: ahead.

■[先生(せんせい)] teacher

77

生

■[セイ, ショウ] life; [い(きる), い(ける)] to live, be alive; [い(かす)] to revive, let live; [う(まれる)] to be born; [う(む)] to give birth; [お(う), は(える), は(やす)] to grow; [き] pure; [なま] raw

■ Again we have a sprout or new leaf of grass on top, as in *sen* above, but this time it is combined with the character for earth or soil [土]. Just as a sprout emerges by pushing through the soil, this kanji means to be born or to come into existence.

■[生徒(せいと)] student, pupil

78

■[ホク; きた] north

■Now come four kanji that are easy to confuse. The first is based on the shape of two people sitting back to back. And how do people's backs relate to the idea of north? Simple—people tend to face south because it is generally sunnier (hence the preference for south-facing rooms), which means that their backs are more likely to be turned northward.

■[北口(きたぐち)] north exit

79

比

■[ヒ] ratio, comparison; [くら(べる)] to compare

■Instead of back to back, this time we have two people sitting in line. This gives rise to the meaning of this kanji, comparison, based on the concept that when two people are lined up next to one another, they will naturally start to compare themselves with each other.

■[比較(ひかく)] comparison; [比々谷(ひびや)] Hibiya (district of Tokyo)

80

化

■[カ, ケ; ば(ける)] to turn into or take the form of something else; [ば(かす)] to bewitch

■The combination of a person standing [亻] and sitting [匕] conveys the idea of someone changing their posture, from which comes the meaning of this kanji: changing form.

■[文化(ぶんか)] culture

81

花

■[カ; はな] flower

■The last kanji of this group has the radical *kusakanmuri* [艹] on top, which is based on the shape of two young shoots sprouting from the soil, and used in words related to plants, especially grasses and flowering plants. Combined with *ka* [化] underneath, denoting a change of form, we have young shoots changing form; that is, coming into bloom.

■[花見(はなみ)] flower viewing (especially cherry blossoms); [花火(はなび)] fireworks

82

名

■[メイ, ミョウ; な] name

■Now we come to a kanji combining the character *yū* [夕], on top, meaning evening, with *kuchi* [口], or mouth, below. In past times it was customary, when people came across one another after dark, to identify themselves by exchanging names.

■[名前(なまえ)] name

83

■[カク; おのおの] each, every; various

■This kanji can be distinguished from the preceding one by the longer right-hand stroke in its upper element. It may help to imagine this stroke pointing to each article in a group of objects. The roots of this character lie in the concept of different words coming out of the mouths of different people, leading to its meanings: each, every or various.

■[各国(かっこく)] each/every country; various countries

84

■[カイ, エ] meeting; [あ(う)] to meet

■ The top element [𠆢] of this kanji conveys the idea of people gathering, and the lower character [云] used to mean to say or to speak. Putting these together, we have the concept of people gathering together and talking.

■[会話(かいわ)] conversation

85

■[ゴウ, ガッ, カッ; あ(う)] to fit; [あ(わす), あ(わせる)] to put together

■ The lower part here consists of the characters for one [一] and mouth [口]. This signifies people gathering and expressing opinions in harmony with each other, as though they had 'one mouth.'

■[国際連合(こくさいれんごう)] the United Nations

86

■[キン] gold; money; metal; [コン] gold; [かね] money; [かな] metal

■ If you look at the lower part of the middle element you will find the character for ground or earth [土] (see No. 50). This denotes the idea of gold (represented originally by two dots) [⺰] mingled with earth, and by extension, has come to mean money as well as to signify metal in general.

■[金山(きんざん)] gold mine

87

■[ゼン; まった(く)] all, whole, entirely
■ This kanji combines the element that denotes people gathering [𠆢] with the character for king [王] (see No. 116). An easy way to remember that it means all or entirely is to think of a king, as the center of an assembly of people, possessing absolute power.
■[全部(ぜんぶ)] all

88

■[ジュン] 10-day period
■ The outer element [勹] of the next pair signifies to hold or envelop something. Although the only difference between these two kanji is a small horizontal stroke in the center, this is enough to give them quite distinct meanings. The first kanji has the character *hi* [日] (the sun or day), in the center. This conveys the concept of a fixed period; specifically, a period of 10 days.
■[上旬(じょうじゅん)] first / [中旬(ちゅうじゅん)] middle / [下旬(げじゅん)] last 10 days of a month

89

■[ク] phrase, clause, verse
■ This time the character inside the enclosure is *kuchi* [口], meaning mouth. Rather than a period of days, this character signifies a group of verbalized sounds — that is, words — which leads to such associated meanings as phrase, clause, and verse.
■[俳句(はいく)] haiku

90

■[ギュウ; うし] cow, bull

■ And here we have a kanji modeled after the head of a cow or bull. In order to differentiate this character from the next one, *go* [午] (noon), it might help to think of the protruding vertical line in the center here as one of the animal's horns.

■[牛肉(ぎゅうにく)] beef

91

■[ゴ] noon

■ A mortar and pestle form the model for this kanji. The concept here is of transition from one state to another. As the direction of the pestle changes from up to down, so does the day wax and wane, moving from morning to night. Noon, then, is the point where the day crosses from morning to afternoon. In the past, noon was known as the time of the *uma*, or horse. So in a corollary to the comment for *ushi* (cow) above, remember that the central vertical line does not protrude upwards in this kanji just as a horse doesn't have horns.

■[午前(ごぜん)] morning; [午後(ごご)] afternoon

92

■[ハン; なか(ば)] half

■In former days this kanji was written [半], with the top element [八] indicating to divide something. The lower part [牛] is an abbreviated form of *ushi* [牛], meaning cow or bull. The origin of this character comes from the idea of 'dividing' (butchering) a cow into two, giving the concept of half. As an aid to remembering it, see how the vertical line protruding from the top bisects the character into two halves.

■[半分(はんぶん)] half

93

■[ヨウ; ひつじ] sheep

■The fact that this character represents the head of a sheep may not be immediately apparent. To distinguish it from *ushi* [牛], meaning cow or bull, remember that *hitsuji* has an extra horizontal line (to match its extra-thick coat of wool), and that its horns are symbolized by the two small strokes at the top — rather than the stroke at the left and the protruding vertical line seen in its bovine cousin.

■[羊毛(ようもう)] wool

94

■[ビ] beauty; [うつく(しい)] beautiful

■And when the character *ō(kii)* [大] (see No. 14), meaning large, is placed under [⺷] (a slightly modified version of *hitsuji*), we have the idea of a large sheep as something excellent and beautiful (at least to a farmer!), as well as the extended meaning: delicious.

■[美人(びじん)] beautiful woman; [美味(びみ)] good flavor; a delicacy

95

■[ヘイ, ビョウ; たい(ら), ひら] evenness, flatness; even, level; simple

■ This kanji originated as the symbol for an aquatic weed floating on the surface of a body of water, from which is derived its meaning: flat.

■[平野(へいや)] plain; [平和(へいわ)] peace, harmony

96

■[ライ; く(る), きた(る)] to come; [きた(す)] to bring about

■This common character was derived from a drawing of ears of wheat or a similar grain. One way to remember it is to imagine that the two lower strokes [ヘ] signify fully grown ears of wheat, drooping from the weight of the grain they contain. As wheat is traditionally considered a gift from the gods, the meaning, to come, is associated with 'coming from heaven.'

■[来年(らいねん)] next year

97

■[マツ, バツ; すえ] end

■ With the addition of a slightly longer horizontal line in the upper part of a tree [木], we obtain a symbol of the head or crown of the tree. And this, in turn, signifies the end or farthest extremity of something. As an aid to remembering that the upper horizontal line is the longer of the two, think of a fully grown branch at the top of the tree.

■[週末(しゅうまつ)] weekend

98

■[ミ] not yet

■In contrast to the preceding kanji, here we have a tree with a short horizontal line added to the upper part. This represents the emergence of a new branch which is not yet fully grown. You should have no problem remembering the order of long and short horizontal lines here either; the top branch is obviously shorter because it has not yet grown to maturity.

■[未定(みてい)] undecided, unfixed, unsettled

99

■[シ; や] arrow

■This kanji is based on the shape of an arrow. To distinguish it from the next kanji, *ushina(u)* [失],

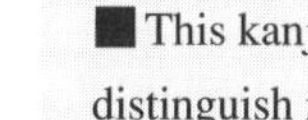

remember that the main vertical stroke [ノ] in this case does not extend beyond the upper horizontal line.

■[弓矢(ゆみや)] a bow and arrow

100

■[シツ; うしな(う)] to lose

■The idea conveyed here is of something slipping out of one's grasp and disappearing. As opposed to the kanji for arrow above, think of the main vertical stroke here slipping through the top so as to extend beyond the upper horizontal line.

■[失敗(しっぱい)] failure

101

■[スイ; みず] water

■Now we come to a group of three kanji centering around the character *mizu* [水], or water. *Mizu* itself is modeled, of course, on a flowing body of water such as a stream or river.

■[水道(すいどう)] water supply

102

■[ヒョウ; こおり, ひ] ice

■To differentiate this kanji from *mizu*, a useful device might be to think of the small stroke [丶] at the top left here as representing a chunk of ice.

■[氷水(こおりみず)] ice water

103

■[エイ; なが(い)] long (time), eternal

■The third member of this group is in the form of a river confluence. Just as a river with all its tributaries flows continuously over a long distance, time moves relentlessly onward. There are two small points of difference between this character and *mizu* [水]: the central vertical line starts with a short horizontal stroke from the left [亅], and there is a small stroke [丶] directly above this vertical line.

■[永住(えいじゅう)] permanent residence

104

馬

■[バ; うま, ま] horse

■The model for this kanji is a horse, which is exactly what the character signifies. The four small strokes at the bottom [灬] represent the horse's legs.

■[馬車(ばしゃ)] horse-drawn carriage; [馬鹿(ばか)] fool, idiot

105

鳥

■[チョウ; とり] bird

■And this kanji takes its form from the shape of a bird. To help differentiate it from *uma* [馬] above, think of the long horizontal line protruding from the central stem as one of the bird's wings. You could also imagine the small slanting dash at the top left to be the bird's beak. In this case, the four small strokes at the bottom represent the bird's feet, rather than four legs.

■[小鳥(ことり)] a small bird

106

■[トウ; しま] island

■This kanji combines the character for bird with that for mountain [山]. A small mountain in the ocean where migratory birds stop to rest would, of course, be an island.

■[半島(はんとう)] peninsula

107

■[カ] good; approval; possible

■ Formed by combining a mouth [口] with something that is convoluted or bent [丁], this kanji was derived from the concept of someone shouting '*yoshi*!' (good!) after having succeeded in a difficult task, and so means to give approval and to be possible.

■[可能(かのう)] possible, practicable; [許可(きょか)] permission

108

■[カ; なに, なん] what; which; how many (interrogative prefix)

■ On the left is *ninben* [亻], denoting a person, while on the right is the character [可], which in this case signifies the concept of goodness. This combination, of course, means a good person. The roots of this kanji lie in the interesting perception that when one sees a person who is good or great in some way, the natural reaction is to wonder what sort of person he or she is, and how that person became that way. This kanji is therefore used to convey interrogatives such as what, which, and how. Be careful not to join the left and right elements together at the top, or you will create a character similar to the kanji [向] described in No. 110.

■[何時(なんじ)] what time

109

■[カ, ガ; かわ] river

■Here, the radical *sanzui* [氵] (water) is added to the left of *ka* (No. 107). This signifies a river so large that even if one shouts loudly from one bank, one's voice will not be heard from the other side. (One reading of this kanji is *kawa*; take care not to confuse it with [川], which has the same reading but is used to mean river in a more general sense. Note that [川], not [河], is used in the names of rivers.)

■[運河(うんが)] canal, waterway; [氷河(ひょうが)] glacier

110

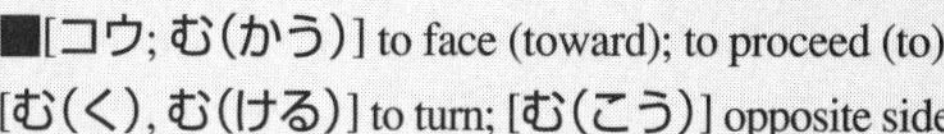

■[コウ; む(かう)] to face (toward); to proceed (to); [む(く), む(ける)] to turn; [む(こう)] opposite side

■This kanji depicts a window of a house. Windows are usually installed to face either north-south or east-west so as to allow the breeze to blow unimpeded through the house. This leads to such meanings as to turn or to face, as well as meaning the opposite side.

■[方向(ほうこう)] direction, way, course

111

■[ドウ; おな(じ)] same

■Here we have a kanji derived from the shape of a round hole drilled through a square block of wood. As the width of the hole does not vary throughout the block, this character symbolizes things that are the same.

■[同時(どうじ)] simultaneous, at the same time

112

■[カ; に] a load, burden, cargo

■ The radical on top here is *kusakanmuri* [艹], signifying grasses or flowering plants, below which is the character [何] which signifies a good person. A good person will no doubt be a hard worker, carrying plenty of grass (perhaps harvested grains) from the fields. Hence, this kanji means shouldering a burden, or the load or burden itself.

■[荷物(にもつ)] baggage, luggage

113

■[フ; つ(く)] to be attached, stick to, belong; [つ(ける)] to attach, stick on

■ On the left here is the radical *ninben* [亻], meaning person, while the character [寸] on the right represents a hand. This combination signifies touching another person with one's hand, from which the meanings to attach or to stick to something, as well as to give, have evolved.

■[受付(うけつけ)] reception desk; [寄付(きふ)] contribution, donation

114

■[フ] government office; center

■ With the addition of [广], signifying a building, to the preceding kanji, the core meaning becomes a storehouse where things are closely packed together. In olden times, storehouses were used primarily to hold rice, particularly that which was levied as taxes by the local ruler or the government. Thus this kanji also means a government office.

■[政府(せいふ)] government

115

■[フ] sign, mark

■ The top radical here is *takekanmuri* [⺮], meaning bamboo. In the past, before paper became common, agreements were often written on strips of bamboo which were then divided in two — one half being kept as a form of proof by the party on each side of the transaction. From this system came the present-day meaning: sign or mark.

■[切符(きっぷ)] ticket

116

王

■[オウ] king

■ This kanji portrays a great person standing upright between the sky and the earth and so, by implication, a king or monarch.

■[王様(おうさま)] king

117

玉

■[ギョク; たま] jewel; round object

■ The origin of this kanji is a string of jewels, such as a necklace or bracelet, linked by a thread. The small stroke [丶] at the right differentiates this kanji from *ō* (king) above.

■[目玉(めだま)] eyeball

118

宝

■[ホウ; たから] treasure, riches

■Here we have a combination of the radical *ukanmuri* [宀], denoting the roof of a house, and the character *tama* [玉] described above, signifying a jewel. The depiction of a house containing jewels leads to the meaning of this kanji: treasure.

■[宝石(ほうせき)] precious stone, gem

119

■[シュ, ス; ぬし, おも] master, owner; main, principal

■Based on a candlestick with a flame burning at the top, this kanji signifies a firmly rooted central point which illuminates its surroundings. Its meanings, the master or head of a household, as well as the main or principal object among several, are derived from this. Remember the small stroke [丶] at the top which represents a flame and distinguishes this kanji from the others in this group.

■[主人(しゅじん)] head (of a family), husband, proprietor, host

120

■[ジュウ] dwelling; [す(む), す(まう)] to live, dwell

■On the left is the radical *ninben* [亻], denoting a person, while on the right is the character [主], whose core meaning is to be firmly rooted. This combination signifies a fixed dwelling or house, and by extension, the concept of living in a certain place.

■[住所(じゅうしょ)] address

121

往

■[オウ] to go

■ This time, the radical on the left is *gyōninben* [彳], which signifies travel along a path or road. This makes it easy to distinguish this kanji from *su(mu)* [住], above.

■[往復(おうふく)] round trip

122

■[チュウ] note, comment; [そそ(ぐ)] to pour, concentrate on, flow

■ From the combination of *sanzui* [氵] (water) on the left and convergence toward a fixed or central point [主] on the right, we derive the concept of rivers emptying into the ocean. This leads to meanings such as pouring and concentrating, as well as to take note of something.

■[注意(ちゅうい)] caution, warning

123

■[チュウ] to stop, stay

■ Here we have the radical *umahen* [馬], meaning horse, on the left, and again the concept of being firmly rooted on the right. The image derived from this combination is of a horse in a stable or corral, perhaps at a town along one of the old highways, implying the act of stopping or staying the night.

■[駐車場(ちゅうしゃじょう)] parking lot

124

駅

■[エキ] station

■Again, [馬] is on the left, and on the right is a modification of a character that once meant to change. In the past, horses were made ready at post towns, or *shukuba*, along major highways so travelers could exchange a tired mount for a fresh one at each stage of their journey. These towns were also called *eki*. Although modern travelers will be changing trains rather than horses, the basic meaning of this kanji is still the same.

■[駅前(えきまえ)] in front of the station

125

■[ヤク] translation; [わけ] reason, meaning; circumstances

■The radical *gonben* [言] on the left here is associated with words or speaking, and on the right again is the modified version of the character meaning to change. This combination signifies changing difficult expressions into those that can be more easily understood, or the process of translation, and by extension, reason or meaning itself.

■[翻訳(ほんやく)] translation

126

■[カイ; こころよ(い)] pleasant, refreshing

■Here we have the radical *risshinben* [忄] on the left, meaning *kokoro* (usually translated as heart in the spiritual or emotional sense). On the right is [夬], which has been modified by trimming the left-hand vertical stroke from the character [中] and adding the representation of a hand. All this symbolizes a heart that is open, as if a part has been trimmed off by hand, and filled with pleasant or refreshing feelings.

■[快速(かいそく)] rapid (train)

127

■[ケツ; き(める)] to decide; [き(まる)] to be decided

■Instead of *kokoro* on the left here we have the radical *sanzui* [氵] signifying water, giving the overall analogy of a riverbank broken by a flood. This original connotation of breaking has evolved into the concept of deciding; perhaps it might help to think of a decision as cutting incisively to the root of a problem, or of breaking through to a solution.

■[決定(けってい)] decision

128

■[オウ] center, middle

■This is an easy kanji to decipher, as it depicts a person in the middle of a frame. This expresses the idea of something being at the center.

■[中央(ちゅうおう)] center, middle

129

■[エイ] excellent, brilliant; England

■The combination of *kusakanmuri* [艹], used in words related to plants, especially grasses and flowering plants, and [央], which is described above and means center, creates the concept of a plant with a splendid flower blooming at the center. Hence the connotation of excellence or brilliance. Later, this character also came to mean England; British readers, at least, will find this association with excellence appropriate.

■[英雄(えいゆう)] hero; [英語(えいご)] the English language

130

■[ホ, ブ, フ; ある(く), あゆ(む)] to walk

■The upper element [止] here means to stop, while below is the character [少] (see No. 13), meaning little or not much. An easy way to differentiate this kanji from similar characters is to think of someone walking a long distance on foot and stopping very little en route.

■[歩道(ほどう)] sidewalk

131

■[ソウ; はし(る)] to run

■In this kanji the upper element [土] represents the earth or the ground, while the lower part [龰] has the appearance of a person moving with long strides. Combined, these elements denote the concept of running on the ground.

■[逃走(とうそう)] escape, getaway

132

■[ソク; あし] foot, leg; [た(りる), た(る)] to be sufficient; [た(す)] to add

■Believe it or not, this kanji depicts a leg. The upper part, which looks like the character for mouth [口], in fact signifies the kneecap or the knee itself. Other meanings associated with this kanji are to be sufficient and to add. Think of the legs as a useful addition to the body, making it sufficiently mobile.

■[足首(あしくび)] ankle; [満足(まんぞく)] satisfaction

133

■[シャ; くるま] wheel; vehicle

■This kanji has the outline of a carriage or chariot, as shown in the accompanying diagram. From this comes its present-day use in words associated with wheels, vehicles and various forms of transportation.

■[電車(でんしゃ)] train

134

■[ジ, ズ; こと] thing, matter

■Here we have a character with rather mysterious origins, depicting a fortuneteller holding a stick or rod in the hand for the purpose of divination. Extending from its sense of the vocation of fortuneteller, this character came to mean job or matter in general or, simply, a thing.

■[工事(こうじ)] construction

135

■[ショ; か(く)] to write

■Instead of a divining stick or rod, as in the previous character, this kanji represents a hand using a brush to write characters on a sheet of paper. Hence its meaning, to write, and its associated connotations which include things that are written, such as books.

■[書道(しょどう)] calligraphy; [書店(しょてん)] bookstore

136

■[レツ] a row, line

■Although it is difficult to imagine at first glance, the left-hand element of this kanji signifies animal bones that have been chopped into pieces. With the radical *rittō* [刂] on the right, representing a sword, we have the concept of cutting up bones of a butchered animal and arranging them neatly with the meat, signifying things being in a row or lining up. This kanji often appears in signs on station platforms.

■[二列(にれつ)] two lines (e.g., in a queue)

137

例

■[レイ] example, custom, precedent; [たと(える)] to compare

■The combination of *ninben* [亻], meaning person, and the character *retsu* [列] described above, meaning a row or a line, suggests people queuing up in lines. This, in turn, has come to include meanings associated with friends or colleagues, things that are similar to each other, and things being as usual.

■[例外(れいがい)] exception

138

■[カン] main part; [みき] trunk (of a tree)

■On the left here, the sun is depicted rising through stalks of grass [龺], while the right-hand element signifies a thick pillar or pole [干] surmounted by a fluttering flag or banner [𠆢]. This combination represents a strong tree trunk rising like the sun and, as a corollary, indicates something that is at the center or core.

■[新幹線(しんかんせん)] the Shinkansen

139

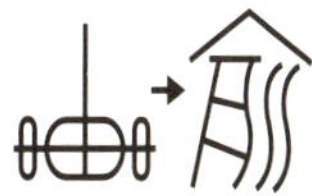

■[ユ] to send, transport

■The structure of this kanji is a little involved, but there is a certain logic to it all. The radical on the left, *kurumahen* [車], means wheel or vehicle (see No. 133). Turning our attention to the right-hand element, the top part [亼] represents the idea of gathering, the part on the lower left [⺝] depicts a boat, and the part on the lower right [刂] was formerly written [巜], representing a river. Integrating these three parts on the right we have boats gathering on a river, signifying the transportation of goods via waterways. And when combined with *kurumahen* on the left, the meaning expands to encompass transportation by other means such as wheeled vehicles.

■[輸入（ゆにゅう）] import; [輸出（ゆしゅつ）] export

140

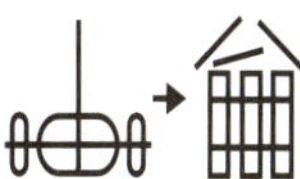

■[リン; わ] wheel, ring, circle

■As in the preceding kanji, the upper part [亼] of the right-hand element means gathering, while the lower part [冊] is derived from the appearance of *tanzaku*, strips of fancy paper traditionally used for writing haiku or tanka poetry which are tied together in neat rows. The right-hand elements thus combine to symbolize the act of gathering things together and neatly arranging or aligning them. With *kurumahen* again on the left, this kanji signifies the wheels of a cart held together by a central axle, and by analogy, objects shaped like a ring or circle.

■[車輪（しゃりん）] wheel; [指輪（ゆびわ）] (finger) ring

141

■[ジョ] slowly

■This kanji is a combination of *gyōninben* [彳] on the left, signifying travel along a path or road, and the element [余] on the right, meaning left over or having room for something. Together, these elements have come to mean walking or moving along slowly, taking plenty of time. The expression shown in the example below can often be seen on signs lining expressways.

■[徐行(じょこう)] proceed slowly

142

■[ジョ, ジ; のぞ(く)] to get rid of, exclude

■The left-hand radical here, *kozatohen* [阝], signifies a hill or mound formed by piles of earth, while on the right we again see the element [余] symbolizing the state of being left over. The overall meaning thus becomes to get rid of spare soil or, for that matter, anything else that is unwanted.

■[除雪(じょせつ)] snow clearing; [大掃除(おおそうじ)] a cleanup

143

■[ケイ, ギョウ; かたち, かた] shape, form

■On the left here is a stylized representation of a square frame [开], while the strokes on the right symbolize a traditional hair ornament such as women used to wear. This combination means shape or form. Although the main purpose of a hair ornament would normally be for decoration, you could also think of it as a way to give shape or form to the hair.

■[形容詞(けいようし)] adjective; [人形(にんぎょう)] doll

144

型

■[ケイ; かた] type, model, mold

■Once again the square frame appears on the top left, and to its right is one of the representations for sword or knife [刂]. Underneath these is the character for earth, ground or soil [土], giving a clue to its overall meaning: using a knife to sculpt an earthen mold to make castings. And as a mold is used to produce a succession of identical objects, this kanji also conveys the idea of an original form or model.

■[大型車(おおがたしゃ)] large-sized car

145

■[シン; おや] parent; [した(しい)] intimate, familiar, friendly; [した(しむ)] to get to know better

■The left-hand character here is a combination of [立], meaning to stand, and [木], meaning tree, while on the right is [見], which means seeing or watching. And what would parents of yore be expected to do? Why, to stand on the upper branches of a tree so as to watch over their children, of course.

■[両親(りょうしん)] parents

146

■[シン; あたら(しい), あら(た), にい] new, afresh

■On the right this time is a character depicting an axe [斤]. This kanji's overall meaning, new, is derived from the implication of a tree that has just been felled by an axe.

■[新聞(しんぶん)] newspaper

147

■[キン; ちか(い)] near

■The radical on the left here is *shinnyō* [⻌], meaning to travel along a path or road or to advance, while on the right the representation of an axe again appears. The sound of wood being chopped can only be heard from nearby, and so this kanji means near.

■[近所(きんじょ)] neighborhood, vicinity

148

■[ショ; ところ] place

■On the left this time is the character for door [戸], while an axe appears again on the right. Just as the sound of wood being chopped indicates the spot where a tree is being felled or cut up, this kanji means place or location.

■[住所(じゅうしょ)] address

149

■[ドウ, トウ; みち] road, street, path

■Now we come to a group of five kanji with the left-hand radical *shinnyō* [⻌], meaning to travel along a path or road or to advance. The first member of this group has the element [首] (see No. 6) on the right, which denotes the neck or the head. Once, if one saw people's heads moving along, though their bodies might be obscured by crops or by tall grass, one could be sure that they were following a road or path.

■[東海道(とうかいどう)] the Tōkaidō Highway

150

■[ツウ, ツ; とお(る)] to pass, go through; [とお (す)] to let through, put through; [かよ(う)] to commute, to run (train, etc.)

■In this case, the right-hand character represents a person squatting down [マ], and piercing a board with a nail [用] (see No. 73). In combination with *shinnyō* again on the left, this kanji signifies a road penetrating or passing through an area without obstruction.

■[山手通り(やまてどお)り] Yamate-dōri

151

週

■[シュウ] week

■The character on the right here combines a modified form of [用], meaning to use, and [口], meaning mouth. This indicates that, in order to inform people of something, the mouth must be used to explain it and spread the word. With the addition of *shinnyō* on the left, we obtain the implication of making the rounds or moving in cycles and, by extension, the concept of weeks.

■[今週(こんしゅう)] this week

152

■[ツイ; お(う)] to go after, pursue; to drive away

■In this, the fourth member of the group, the right-hand element [𠂤] represents the shape of a hill. The combination of this element with *shinnyō* on the left creates the idea of pursuing a person who is trying to escape into the hills, which is usually the first place that a fugitive will head. The expression in the example below is often seen in signs along highways.

■[追(お)い越(こ)し] overtaking, passing

153

■[ハク; せま(る)] to press (someone), urge; to approach, draw near

■Take care not to confuse this kanji with the preceding one; the left-hand radical is the same but on the right, instead of [𠂤], we have the similar-looking character *shiro* [白] (see No. 2), meaning white. An easy way to remember the meaning of this kanji is to think of a road that is brightly lit with white light, making it easy to approach and to continue on one's journey.

■[圧迫（あっぱく）] pressure, oppression

154

■[ハク; と(まる)] to stay (overnight); [と(める)] to put somebody up, lodge somebody

■This time the right-hand character is still *shiro*, but the radical on the left is now *sanzui* [氵], symbolizing water. The connotation here is the water's edge, where white waves crash against the shore. In the past, long journeys were likely to be by boat, and when night fell the vessel would be moored by the shore so that those aboard could get a good night's sleep. Hence the meaning of this kanji: to stay overnight.

■[一泊二食付き（いっぱくにしょくつき）] overnight stay with two meals; [停泊（ていはく）] anchorage, mooring

155

■[ケン] ticket, certificate

■The top element [龹] here represents dividing something into two with both hands, while the character [刀], meaning sword, forms the lower element. In the past, two people entering into an agreement or pact would engrave the details on a wooden tablet with a knife or small sword, then cut the tablet into two halves. Each party would keep one of these halves as proof, creating a type of deed. Now this kanji is mostly used to mean ticket.

■[定期券(ていきけん)] commuter ticket (season pass)

156

■[カン; まき] reel, volume (of a book, etc.); a roll; [ま(く)] to roll, to wind

■Again we have [龹] on top, signifying division, while the lower element [己] this time is a modification of [㔾], which depicts a person kneeling and curled up into a ball. Thus, we have a kanji symbolizing division and curling up, or rolling things up into circular form. One place that you will often see this character is in shops selling *norimaki*, the long sushi rolls wrapped in thin sheets of *nori* seaweed. This kanji is also associated with books, reflecting the fact that in former times books were compiled as scrolls.

■[海苔巻(のりまき)] *norimaki*; [第二巻(だいにかん)] Volume 2

157

■[デン; た] rice paddy

■This is an easy one: a kanji modeled after neatly segmented rice fields. In Japan, when used alone, this kanji means an irrigated rice paddy, while in China it can refer to both rice paddies and other types of cultivated fields.

■[田植(たうえ)] rice planting

158

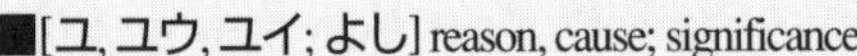

■[ユ, ユウ, ユイ; よし] reason, cause; significance

■Although this kanji looks like *ta* above, but with the central vertical line extending upwards, in fact there is no relationship at all between the two characters. Instead, this kanji depicts the fruit of a tree hanging down from its branches, and expresses such concepts as logic, grasping the reality (the 'fruit') of something, origin, reason, and similar ideas.

■[理由(りゆう)] reason; [自由(じゆう)] freedom

159

■[キョク] curve; melody; [ま(がる)] to turn, be bent, be curved; [ま(げる)] to bend, distort, twist (something)

■This kanji was modeled after a container made by bending wood or bamboo into the desired form, and thus has meanings related to bending, curving, and turning. It also means melody—to remember this, it might help to think of musical notes floating here and there as they are carried along on the breeze, or of rising and falling intonations.

■[曲線(きょくせん)] a curve; [作曲(さっきょく)] musical composition

160

■[シン; もう(す)] to say; to be named

■Here a vertical line extends above and below the character *ta*, although again there is no association with the idea of a field. Originally, this kanji represented something stretching over a long distance (the extended line makes this easy to remember), but this evolved into the idea of expressing one's inner feelings. Hence the current meaning of *mō(su)*: to say or express.

■[申(もう)し上(あ)げる] to say, express; [申告(しんこく)] a report, statement, (tax) return

161

■[シン, ジン; かみ, かん, こう] a god, deity; God

■The next pair of kanji both have *mō(su)* [申] as their right-hand element. In the first of these, the radical on the left is *shimesuhen* [礻], which is based on the shape of an altar and signifies a god or deity. In combination with *mō(su)* (to say) on the right, we have the idea of praying in front of an altar. Thus this character has come to signify the deity itself.

■[神社(じんじゃ)] Shinto shrine; [神道(しんとう)] Shintoism, Shinto; [神様(かみさま)] a god, God

162

■[シン] a man of culture, gentleman

■Here the left-hand radical is *itohen* [糹] (see No. 201), meaning thread. If you read the explanation for *mō(su)* again you'll recall that originally it represented something stretching over a long distance. Combined with *itohen*, the character gains the sense of the large ceremonial sash worn by high officials in past eras. From this, the character came to denote someone of high rank, or a man of culture and dignity.

■[紳士服(しんしふく)] men's clothing

163

細

■[サイ; ほそ(い)] slender, narrow; detailed; [ほそ(る)] to become thinner; [こま(か), こま(かい)] small; detailed

■The radical *itohen* again appears on the left, while the character on the right used to represent the brain and blood vessels and was later modified to [田]. This kanji therefore refers to things that are slender or detailed, like threads or small blood vessels.

■[細道(ほそみち)] narrow road; [細工(さいく)] workmanship

164

畑

■[はたけ, はた] field, farm

■While rice paddies are also referred to as *suiden* [水田]—which literally means 'water field'—because they are irrigated before planting, fields for other crops are traditionally prepared by burning, which clears away any unwanted vegetation and provides ash to fertilize the land. From this practice of burning, the character *hatake* [畑]—meaning 'fire field'—has developed. This character originated in Japan, so it has no *on-yomi*, or Chinese phonetical reading.

■[花畑(はなばたけ)] field of flowers, flower garden

165

■[リョ; たび] journey, trip, travel

■If you think of a group of Japanese people on an organized tour, the image of the tour leader waving a colorful flag will probably spring into your mind. Interestingly enough, this character does actually represent a line of people with a flag flying at the front, leading the way. To distinguish this kanji from the following one, *zoku* [族], remember that the lower right-hand element [⺁] here is a modification of [从], meaning people.

■[旅行(りょこう)] a journey, travel

166

■[ゾク] family, tribe, clan

■This character also contains a depiction of a flag, but now in combination with the character for arrow [矢] (see No. 99) on the lower right. A gathering of arrows under a flag signifies an assembly of members of the same family, tribe or clan.

■[家族(かぞく)] family

167

組

■[ソ; くみ] group, crew, class, gang; [く(む)] to join, put together

■Next we have a pair of similar-looking kanji. In both of these, the character [且] appears on the right, representing a pile of objects stacked on a base or foundation. In the first kanji, the radical on the left is *itohen* [糸], meaning thread. This leads to the concept of things or people being assembled like objects strung together on a thread, with extended meanings such as group, crew, and so on.

■[番組(ばんぐみ)] program; [組織(そしき)] organization, system

168

■[ソ] ancestor

■The left-hand radical here is *shimesuhen* [礻], which is based on the shape of an altar and signifies a god or deity. The combination with [且] on the right symbolizes the accumulation of many generations, or ancestors, which have become venerated as gods.

■[祖先(そせん)] ancestor; [祖母(そぼ)] grandmother

169

■[フク] good fortune, blessing

■Now we have two kanji that sake-lovers will relate to, since both contain [畐] depicting a full bottle of sake or other liquor and, by extension, signifying wealth or assets. In the first kanji, the character symbolizing wealth is on the right and the radical *shimesuhen* [礻], meaning a god or deity, is on the left. A person on whom the gods bestow wealth is indeed blessed with good fortune and happiness.

■[幸福(こうふく)] happiness

170

副

■[フク] vice-, sub-, secondary

■This time, the symbol for wealth is on the left, and the radical *rittō* [刂], representing a sword, is on the right. The symbolism here is dividing wealth or assets into two, with half being spare or held in reserve in case of emergency. Hence this character came to mean secondary, as seen in prefixes such as those listed above.

■[副大統領(ふくだいとうりょう)] vice-president; [副都心(ふくとしん)] subcenter of a metropolis

171

■[サイ; まつ(り)] festival; [まつ(る)] to deify, worship

■Here, the top left element [⺼] is modeled on a piece of meat, while beside it is the representation of a right hand [⺕]. The third element [示], forms the base, and symbolizes an altar. The overall meaning is thus to offer animal meat at an altar, which leads to the extended meanings to deify or to worship a deity and, because it is essentially a religious observance, a festival.

■[春祭り(はるまつり)] spring festival

172

■[サツ] to guess, perceive, sympathize

■Here we have the preceding kanji, *matsu(ri)* [祭], meaning festival, surmounted by the radical *ukanmuri* [宀], denoting the roof of a house. This combination signifies a festival in honor of one's ancestors, an event of great importance. From this comes the nuance of carefully checking or perceiving things.

■[警察(けいさつ)] police

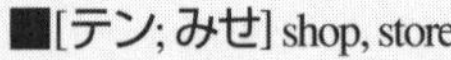

173

店

■[テン; みせ] shop, store

■This kanji has two parts: the radical *madare* [广] (a building) above, and [占] (fortunetelling) below. As one might guess, [口] (mouth) is integral to the character for fortune-telling. Add to this the fact that a shop used to be part of a merchant's home, and we reach the roots of this kanji: having goods for sale at one's home and chatting to shoppers, just as fortunetellers ply their trade by talking to customers.

■[店員(てんいん)] shop assistant; [商店街(しょうてんがい)] shopping street

174

■[オク; や] roof; house; shop

■The upper element [尸] of this kanji depicts a person lying down, while the lower element [至] symbolizes a bird coming to land on the ground, signifying to come or to stay. The concept of a person coming to stay extends this character's meaning to a house or dwelling, and by extension, a shop or store.

■[屋根(やね)] roof; [本屋(ほんや)] bookstore

175

■[シツ] room; [むろ] greenhouse; cellar

■This kanji shares the same origins and has a similar meaning to [屋] above . Here the radical *ukanmuri* [宀], denoting the roof of a house, is on top, with [至] (to come or stay) below. This again leads to the idea of a person coming to stay at one's home, but here the core meaning is a room. The best way to distinguish [室] from [屋] may be to memorize that the kanji with *ukanmuri* (a roof) on top is the one that means room.

■[和室(わしつ)] Japanese-style room; [教室(きょうしつ)] classroom

176

■[ドウ] temple, hall

■The upper part of this kanji [⺌冖] represents smoke issuing from the window of a house, with the nuances of expanding and rising high into the sky, leading to the concept of a building of large dimensions. When this is added to the character [土], representing ground or earth, the overall meaning becomes a large structure, such as a temple or hall, standing on a foundation.

■[本堂 (ほんどう)] main hall (of a temple)

177

■[クウ; そら] sky; empty; [から] empty; [あ(く)] to become empty, vacant; [あ(ける)] to empty, vacate

■The upper radical of this kanji is *anakanmuri* [穴], representing a hole, while the lower element [工] signifies a tool. When one uses a tool to make a hole in something, the result is also the creation of an empty space. And, extending from the concept of emptiness, this kanji also means sky.

■[空手 (からて)] karate; [青空 (あおぞら)] blue sky; [空車 (くうしゃ)] vacant (taxi)

178

■[キュウ; きわ(める)] to study, investigate thoroughly

■Again *anakanmuri* is on top, depicting a hole, but on the bottom this time is the character *kyū* [九] (see No. 25), which represents the number 9. The character for 9 (the highest numeral) was originally associated with going to the limit or mastering something. Thus we have a combination which literally means to examine a hole or empty space to the maximum extent, that is, to investigate something thoroughly.

■[研究 (けんきゅう)] research

179

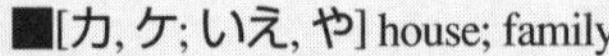

■[カ, ケ; いえ, や] house; family

■The next five kanji are all topped by the radical *ukanmuri* [宀] which represents the roof of a house. The character [豕] under the roof in the first kanji symbolizes a pig. Pigs have always been valuable domestic animals and traditionally, in China, almost every house would have kept one or more of them. Hence its meaning, house, and by association, family.

■[大家 (おおや)] landlord, landlady; [家具 (かぐ)] furniture

180

■[アン; やす(い)] easy, peaceful; cheap

■Here we have *ukanmuri* combined with *onna* [女] (woman). This signifies that when a woman is in the house, looking after things, one can feel at ease. As we all know, women were once supposed to stay in the home while the menfolk worked outside. An easy way to remember this character's additional meaning, cheap, is to think of how easy and peaceful life is when one is able to buy goods cheaply.

■[安心 (あんしん)] peace of mind; [安全 (あんぜん)] safety, security

181

■[タク] house, home, residence

■This time, the character [乇] under the roof signifies grass taking root in the earth and sprouting. This leads to the the concept of settling down in a house, and from this comes the meaning home or dwelling.

■[住宅 (じゅうたく)] house, housing; [宅急便 (たっきゅうびん)] door-to-door delivery

182

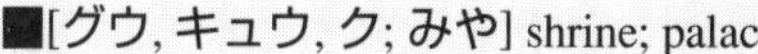

■[グウ, キュウ, ク; みや] shrine; palace

■ And this kanji joins *ukanmuri* with the lower element [呂], which represents a number of rooms in a row. This combination therefore denotes a large mansion, the palace or residence of the Emperor, or a shrine.

■[神宮 (じんぐう)] higher ranking Shinto shrine; [宮殿 (きゅうでん)] palace

183

■[カン] government, authorities

■ The lower element [㠯] in the fifth member of this group is quite similar to that in *miya* above, but notice that the two squares are connected slightly differently. In this case, the lower element depicts an earthen wall. The overall concept thus becomes an imposing house surrounded by such a wall and so, by association, a government office. This kanji is also used in words associated with government or authorities.

■[外交官 (がいこうかん)] diplomat; [官庁 (かんちょう)] government office (agency)

184

■[カン] to control; pipe; wind instrument; [くだ] tube, pipe

■ This kanji consists of *kan* [官], described above, with the radical *takekanmuri* [⺮], meaning bamboo, on top. This combination signifies a bamboo flute, based on the idea that, just as a government office performs its role as determined by the beaureaucracy, so a flute produces sounds as determined by its design. And, by extension, this kanji is associated with tubes and pipes in general, as well as with the concept of control.

■[水道管 (すいどうかん)] water pipe, water main; [管理人 (かんりにん)] caretaker

185

■[シ] city; [いち] market

■The top element of this kanji was formerly the character [止], meaning to stop, while the lower part [巾] symbolizes cloth. Together, they signify a place where people would stop to buy and sell cloth, leading this character to the two meanings: market and city.

■[骨(こっ)とう市(いち)] antique market

186

■[フ] cloth; spreading; [ぬの] (a) cloth

■The lower element here in itself represents cloth, with the addition of the horizontal and slanting lines [ナ] signifying to spread such cloth out. As a corollary, this kanji also means to disseminate or spread something widely.

■[財(さい)布(ふ)] purse, wallet

187

■[ト, ツ; みやこ] capital (city), metropolis

■Next we have a group of three kanji, each of which has the radical *ōzato* [阝], signifying the enclosure of a village or town, on the right. In the first of these kanji, the character on the left is *mono* [者], signifying person or people. Thus combined, these two elements symbolize a large town or capital city where many people gather.

■[都(と)市(し)] city

188

部

■[ブ] part, section, department; copy (of a document, newspaper, etc.)

■ At the top left this time is the character *tatsu* [立], meaning to stand, under which is *kuchi* [口], or mouth. This conveys the idea of opinions being divided in two. With the addition of *ōzato* on the right, we have the concept of dividing a village or town, and by extension, dividing anything into its constituent parts.

■[部分(ぶぶん)] part, section, portion

189

郡

■[グン] county, district

■ The third member of this trio has the character *kun* [君] on the left, meaning a ruler or monarch. With *ōzato* again on the right, this kanji refers to a locality where a community has developed, centered around a ruler. These days it is used to define the administrative subdivisions of a prefecture.

■[郡部(ぐんぶ)] rural district

190

■[グン; む(れ), むら] group, crowd; [む(れる), むら(がる)] to crowd, flock together

■ This time, *kun* on the left is joined by *hitsuji* [羊] (see No. 93), the character for sheep, on the right. The meaning here is all too obvious: sheep tend to group around a leader, thus forming a flock.

■[群島(ぐんとう)] group of islands, archipelago

191

■[テイ; にわ] garden

■The next four kanji are all characterized by the radical *madare* [广], which represents a building. In the first of these, the inner element [廷] symbolizes a person strolling across a flat area. And, of course, a flat area that is next to a building, such as a house, is usually a garden.

■[庭園(ていえん)] garden, park; [中庭(なかにわ)] courtyard

192

■[セキ] seat, place

■The inner element of this kanji has slightly complicated roots, but the logic is quite clear. The upper part [廿] is actually the old way of writing *ni-jū* [二十], which these days means the number 20, but formerly simply expressed the concept of many. The lower part [巾] means cloth. In total, the inner element symbolizes matting made of many cloths; namely, a *zabuton*, or Japanese-style cushion. And in combination with *madare* we have the concept of cushions arranged in a house, leading to such meanings as a place to sit or a seat. (Note that the following kanji also expresses the concept of seat, but has a different etymology.)

■[客席(きゃくせき)] seat (in a theater, taxi, train, etc.); [出席(しゅっせき)] presence, attendance

193

座

■[ザ] seat; theater; constellation; [すわ(る)] to sit
■ This time, the inner element [坐] depicts two people sitting on the ground, facing each other. In combination with *madare*, this creates the concept of sitting in a house or a building such as a theater, and its extended meanings include both seat and the action of sitting.
■[歌舞伎座(かぶきざ)] kabuki theater; [座禅(ざぜん)] Zen meditation

194

度

■[ド, ト, タク] degree; measure; times; [たび] times
■ In the fourth kanji of this group, the inner element consists of [廿] on top, which signifies many (as we have just seen in No. 192), and [又] underneath, representing the right hand. Together these elements denote the act of measuring many things with one's right hand, and the incorporation of the radical *madare* indicates that this includes measuring the dimensions of houses or other buildings. And, reflecting the concept of many measurements being made, this kanji has also come to mean times (as in once, twice, three times, etc.).
■[温度(おんど)] temperature; [今度(こんど)] this time, now; next time; recently

195

■[ゲン] original, fundamental; field; [はら] plain, field, wilderness

■ The radical *gandare* [厂] in this kanji represents a cliff, beneath which is a modified form of the character *izumi* [泉], meaning a spring. The image conveyed here is of a spring flowing out onto the plains from under a cliff, leading to such meanings as field, plain, and wilderness.

■[高原(こうげん)] plateau, highlands

196

■[ゲン; みなもと] source, origin

■ With the addition of *sanzui* [氵] (water) on the left, the idea of a spring as a source of water is highlighted. This is therefore the core meaning of this kanji. As well as meaning source, this kanji means the beginning or the origin.

■[資源(しげん)] resource(s); [震源地(しんげんち)] epicenter (of an earthquake)

197

■[リョウ] material; fee, charge

■ The character for rice is the left-hand radical *komehen* [米] here, while [斗] on the right is in the shape of a scoop or ladle used as a measure. From the concept of measuring come the meanings materials, fee and charge. To distinguish this kanji from *ka* [科], next, it may help to keep in mind that, just as rice is the mainstay of Japanese food (*Nihon ryōri*), the radical *komehen* is the mainstay of the kanji *ryō*.

■[料理(りょうり)] cuisine, cooking; [料金(りょうきん)] fee, charge, fare

198

■[カ] (academic) course, branch, department

■On the left is the radical *nogihen* [禾], based on the shape of an ear of rice or some other cereal. With the character for a measure [斗] on the right, again the root meaning is measuring grain. The extended meanings of this kanji include to check and classify things according to type, as well as the individual categories into which things are sorted.

■[内科(ないか)] (department of) internal medicine; [外科(げか)] (department of) surgery

199

■[ロウ] old age; [お(いる), ふ(ける)] to grow old

■You might have to use your imagination a little, but this kanji is actually modeled after the shape of an old man with long hair and a bent back, supporting himself with a stick.

■[老人(ろうじん)] old person; the elderly

200

■[コウ] thought, idea, opinion; [かんが(える)] to think, consider

■This kanji is basically the same as the previous one, except for an extra twist at the bottom. Interestingly, the idea here is that the meandering thoughts of an old person are deeper than those of their younger counterparts, and thus get to the bottom of things. From this come its meanings, to think or to consider, as well as the concepts of thought, ideas, and opinions in general.

■[思考(しこう)] thought, consideration; [考古学(こうこがく)] archaeology

201

■[シ; いと] thread

■ Although it may not be immediately obvious, this kanji actually depicts filaments of raw silk being twisted together into a thread as they are drawn from the silkworm cocoon.

■[ぬい糸(いと)] sewing thread; [製糸業(せいしぎょう)] the silk-reeling industry

202

■[ケイ] system; lineage; group

■ The addition of an extra stroke [一] to the top of the preceding kanji signifies being connected by a thread, or simply the state of being linked in some way.

■[系列(けいれつ)] system; affiliate; [家系(かけい)] family lineage

203

■[ケイ; かか(る)] to relate to; [かかり] duty; person in charge

■ Combining *ninben* [亻] (person), on the left, with the preceding kanji (signifying connection), on the right, this character denotes being connected or related to other people.

■[関係(かんけい)] relationship, involvement; [案内係(あんないがかり)] desk clerk; usher(ette)

204

■[セン] line

■The left-hand radical this time is *itohen* [糹], meaning thread, while the character [泉] on the right means spring. Together, these two elements signify a long, thin thread, like a watercourse flowing from a spring. This concept has simply come to represent a line.

■[山手線(やまのてせん)] Yamanote Line

205

■[リョク, ロク; みどり] green; greenery

■Although a little difficult to imagine, the element [录] on the right actually depicts shavings of bark lying scattered on the ground. With the addition of *itohen* [糹] on the left, this kanji expresses the idea of thread that has been dyed green—the color of young trees or bamboo shoots after their bark or outer sheath has been peeled off.

■[緑色(みどりいろ)] the color green

206

■[ロク] to copy, write down, record

■On the left this time is the radical *kanehen* [金], meaning metal, and again we see the character representing scattered bark on the right. This kanji signifies characters being engraved on metal, just as they can also be carved into a piece of wood (think of wood shavings, rather than bark, lying scattered). This, in turn, has come to represent both the act of writing characters and that which is recorded.

■[記録(きろく)] record, minutes; [録音(ろくおん)] recording (of music, etc.)

207

話

■[ワ; はなし] story; [はな(す)] to speak

■This kanji has the radical *gonben* [訁] on the left, associated with words or speaking, while on the right is the character *shita* [舌], meaning tongue. These elements doubly reinforce the core meaning here: to speak or to tell a story.

■[電話(でんわ)] telephone

208

■[カツ] life, activity, energy

■The left-hand radical this time is *sanzui* [氵], which signifies water, with the character for tongue appearing again on the right. The concept here is that life can exist provided that there is water and one can eat (symbolized in this case by the tongue).

■[生活(せいかつ)] life, living; [活動(かつどう)] activity, action

209

■[ジ, チ] peace; government; healing; [おさ(める)] to rule over; [おさ(まる)] to be at peace, calm down; [なお(る)] to be healed; [なお(す)] to heal

■Here, *sanzui* (water), on the left, with [台] (a raised foundation that has a view of its surroundings) on the right, signify someone controlling the flow of water from an established foundation or base. The core meaning, government, reflects the fact that flood prevention has always been an important task for rulers.

■[政治(せいじ)] politics

210

■[シ; はじ(める)] to start, begin; [はじ(まる)] to be started

■This time the radical *onnahen* [女], meaning woman, appears on the left, and the character signifying a foundation is once again on the right. Women are the foundation of life, since it is they who give birth to every living being, and from this comes the meaning beginning.

■[開始(かいし)] beginning, opening; [始発(しはつ)] first departure (e.g., train)

211

読

■[ドク, トク, トウ; よ(む)] to read

■The radical *gonben* [言] on the left here is associated with words or speaking, while on the right is the element *u(ru)* [売] (see No. 11), meaning to sell. Traditionally, a person selling wares will call out or talk in a steady monologue to attract customers; from this comes the meaning to read aloud or, simply, to read.

■[読書(どくしょ)] reading; [読者(どくしゃ)] reader, subscriber

212

■[ゾク] continuation; [つづ(く)、つづ(ける)] to continue

■This time the left-hand character is *itohen* [糸], meaning thread, with *u(ru)* (to sell) again on the right. The meaning of this kanji, to continue, is derived from the idea of someone selling their wares for a long time, like a thread stretching over a long distance.

■[手続(てつづ)き] procedure; [連続(れんぞく)] continuance, succession, series

213

説

■[セツ] opinion, theory; [ゼイ; と(く)] to explain, persuade

■Here the radical *gonben* [言], associated with words or speaking, is on the left, while the right-hand element [兑] has three parts: the element [丷] (to open or to divide); *kuchi* [口], (mouth); and *hito* [人] (a person). When these are put together, we have a kanji depicting a person opening their mouth to speak or to explain something, leading to the extended meanings opinion and theory.

■[説明(せつめい)] explanation; [小説(しょうせつ)] novel, story, fiction

214

設

■[セツ; もう(ける)] to establish, set up, prepare

■On the right this time is the radical *rumata* [殳], which signifies a halberd (a type of lance) being held in the hand and, by extension, the use of a tool. When combined with *gonben* on the left, the connotation changes to instructing somebody else to do a job. And from this come such meanings as to make, to establish, and to prepare.

■[建設(けんせつ)] construction; [設備(せつび)] equipment, facilities; accommodation(s)

215

■[ゼイ] tax

■Next the radical *nogihen* [禾], based on an ear of rice or some other cereal, is on the left, and on the right is the combination of three elements, as seen in *setsu* (No. 213), meaning a person opening their mouth. In former times, government officials made regular visits to collect taxes. Even though we no longer use rice to pay taxes, this is a kanji which most of us would still prefer to encounter as little as possible.

■[税金(ぜいきん)] tax; [消費税(しょうひぜい)] consumption tax

216

■[ガク] music; [ラク] pleasure, comfort; [たの(しい)] pleasant, enjoyable; [たの(しむ)] to enjoy

■Here we have a kanji depicting a set of bells and a drum, thus meaning music as well as such derivations as pleasure, comfort, and enjoyment.

■[音楽(おんがく)] music; [楽器(がっき)] musical instrument

217

■[ヤク; くすり] medicine; chemical

■The only difference between this kanji and the preceding one is that the radical *kusakanmuri* [艹] has been added on top. This radical is modeled on the shape of two young shoots sprouting from the soil, and is used in words related to plants, especially grasses and flowering plants. This combination denotes medicinal herbs that provide comfort or relief to the sick, and by extension, chemicals or pharmaceuticals.

■[薬屋(くすりや)] pharmacy, drugstore; [農薬(のうやく)] agricultural chemical

218

若

■[ジャク, ニャク; わか(い)] young, immature; low (number)

■Take care with the next two kanji — they are quite similar in appearance but their meanings are totally different. Both have the upper radical *kusakanmuri*, which, as we have just seen, is used to form words related to plants, especially grasses and flowering plants. In the first member of this pair, the lower character is *migi* [右] (see No. 37), meaning right. From the concept of picking newly sprouted grass with the right hand come such meanings as young, immature, and low in number.

■[若者(わかもの)] young person/people

219

■[ク; くる(しい)] pain; painful, difficult; [くる(しむ)] to suffer, be troubled; [くる(しめる)] to torment, bully; [にが(い)] bitter; [にが(る)] to scowl

■Underneath *kusakanmuri* this time is the character *furu(i)* [古], meaning old. Old grasses — namely, preserved and dried herbs — generally taste bitter. This concept spawns a host of associated meanings related to pain, difficulty, trouble, and other forms of suffering.

■[御苦労様(ごくろうさま)] Thank you for your trouble.

220

■[コウ] school; to correct

■ Now we come to a large group of kanji with the left-hand radical *kihen* [木], meaning tree. The first of these has the character *maji* (*waru*) [交] (see No. 61), signifying to exchange or to associate, on the right. In former times, schools were constructed from wood and their primary function, of course, has always been to instill learning through exchanges between students and teachers.

■[学校(がっこう)] school

221

■[マイ] suffix, counter for thin or flat objects

■ Here, the radical *nobun* [攵] on the right represents a stick or rod held in the hand. This word originally served as a counter for wooden sticks or rods, but now it is used for counting thin or flat objects.

■[十枚(じゅうまい)] ten sheets (of paper, for example)

222

■[リン; はやし] woods, thicket

■ And, logically enough, two trees side by side represent a wooded area or thicket.

■[林道(りんどう)] forestry road

223

■[ソン; むら] village

■ The next kanji in this group has the character [寸] on the right, which means few or little. People gathered to live in places with fewer trees than the thickly forested mountainsides (or perhaps they cut down the nearby trees for firewood and to build houses). This notion of there being few trees where people live explains how this character came to mean village.

■[農村(のうそん)] farm village, rural district

224

■[ザイ] material; timber; ability

■ On the right this time is the shape of a bud protruding slightly from the earth [才], which conveys the concept of a latent function that will be useful in the future. The addition of *kihen* makes the overall meaning of this character wood used for construction and, by extension, raw materials or materials in general.

■[材木(ざいもく)] wood, lumber; [材料(ざいりょう)] materials, ingredients

225

■[ショウ; まつ] pine tree

■ Again we see *kihen* on the left, while on the right is the character *kō* [公], which appears in words such as *kōen* [公園], or park, and signifies something that is public. The association here is that the evergreen pine tree has traditionally been used in public celebrations and formal occasions.

■[松林(まつばやし)] pine grove

226

■[すぎ] Japanese cedar, cryptomeria

■ The three strokes [彡] on the right of this kanji, which are also found in *katachi* [形] (see No. 143), represent a hair ornament such as women traditionally wore. Here they combine with *kihen* to characterize the thin, needle-like foliage of the *sugi*, or Japanese cedar.

■[杉並木 (すぎなみき)] an avenue of Japanese cedar trees

227

■[シ; えだ] branch

■ The next pair of kanji both have the element [支] on the right, signifying a thin twig or shoot held in the hand. (Take care not to confuse this with the radical *nobun* seen in kanji No. 221.) In the first kanji of this pair, the left-hand radical *kihen* reinforces the idea of twigs or boughs branching out from the trunk of a tree.

■[枝ぶり (えだぶり)] the shape of a tree

228

■[ギ; わざ] technique, ability, skill

■ This time the radical on the left is *tehen* [扌], which represents using the hand. This kanji therefore signifies a precise ability or technique, such as is necessary to sort through a bundle of fine twigs.

■[技術 (ぎじゅつ)] technique, technology, skill

229

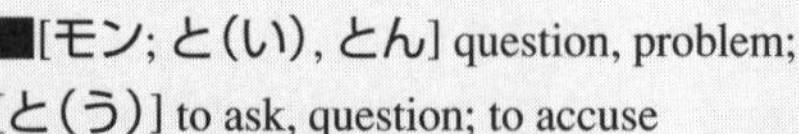

■[モン; と(い), とん] question, problem;
[と(う)] to ask, question; to accuse

■The next four kanji have the enclosing radical *mongamae* [門], representing a *mon*, or gate. The first kanji of this group has *kuchi* [口], meaning mouth, in the middle. The idea here is of bringing one's mouth close to a gate to request entry; hence this kanji means to ask or to question.

■[学問(がくもん)] study, learning; [質問(しつもん)] question, inquiry

230

■[カン, ケン; あいだ] interval; space; [ま] room; interval; time

■Here we see the sun [日] filtering through the portals of a gate, signifying the concept of something being between other things, or an intervening space.

■[時間(じかん)] time; [居間(いま)] living room

231

■[カイ; あ(ける), ひら(く), あ(く)] to open;
[ひら(ける)] to be developed

■The third kanji in this group has [开] in the middle. When riding in an elevator, be careful not to confuse this kanji with the next one [閉], or you may inadvertently close the doors instead of opening them. The key to distinguishing them is to remember that [开] in this kanji symbolizes using both hands to open a latch or lift the crossbar of a gate.

■[開店(かいてん)] opening of a shop; [開会(かいかい)] opening of a meeting

232

■[ヘイ; と(じる), と(ざす), し(める), し(まる)] to shut

■ And [オ] in the middle here signifies a gate that has been closed and locked by inserting vertical and horizontal latches or crossbars. To help distinguish between the kanji for open and close, notice that the middle character in this case is similar to the katakana character *o* [オ]; *o* coincidentally stands for *owari* (end), which implies closing or shutting down.

■[閉店(へいてん)] closing of a shop; [閉会(へいかい)] closing of a meeting

233

■[キョウ, ゴウ; つよ(い)] strong; [つよ(まる)] to become strong; [つよ(める)] to make strong; [し(いる)] to force

■ Again we have a pair of opposites. In the first of these, the radical *yumihen* [弓], meaning a bow (for shooting arrows), is on the left, while the element [虽] on the right is modeled after a hard-shelled beetle. Both of these components are indicative of strength; hence the meaning of this kanji.

■[強力(きょうりょく)] strong, powerful

234

■[ジャク; よわ(い)] weak; [よわ(る), よわ(まる)] to become weak; [よわ(める)] to make weak

■ The second kanji of this pair is shaped like two newly hatched chicks standing side by side. Needless to say, the image of these frail-looking creatures leads to this character's meaning: weak.

■[弱気(よわき)] timid, faint-hearted

235

計

■[ケイ] measuring; plan; total; [はか(る)] to measure, compute; [はか(らう)] to arrange

■ This kanji derives its meaning from the radical *gonben* [言] on the left, which is associated with words or speaking, and the character for the number 10 [十] on the right. The idea depicted here is reciting or chanting numbers out loud, or counting, which has expanded over time into the various meanings listed above.

■[計算（けいさん）] calculation; [計画（けいかく）] plan, project

236

■[シン; はり] needle

■ The left-hand radical this time is *kanehen* [金], meaning metal, while the number 10 is again on the right. The connection between these two elements is rather tenuous, so perhaps the easiest way to remember this kanji is to think of the character [十] as representing a needle (the vertical line) with a thread (the horizontal line) running through its eye.

■[針金（はりがね）] wire; [方針（ほうしん）] policy, course

237

■[カ] fruit, result; [は(たす)] to carry out, fulfill; [は (てる)] to come to an end; [は(て)] end, limit; result

■ Next we have a group of four. The shape of the first kanji in this group signifies fruit on a tree. As a seed represents a new beginning, so fruit symbolizes the end or result.

■[結果（けっか）] result, outcome; [果物（くだもの）] fruit (*Kuda* is a special reading of this kanji, used only for this word.)

238

■[カ] fruit, nut, berry; cake

■ This kanji consists of the radical *kusakanmuri* [艹], representing grasses or flowering plants, on top of the preceding kanji for fruit. Fruits such as Chinese dates and dried apricots have long been popular as snacks in China, and this kanji has therefore acquired an association with refreshments and confectionery.

■[菓子] confectionery, cookies, crackers, etc.

239

■[ソウ; す] nest, lair

■ Take care not to confuse this kanji with the preceding one, *ka*; the upper element here is a representation of young birds in their nest in a tree.

■[巣箱] birdhouse; [巣鴨駅] Sugamo Station (Yamanote Line)

240

■[タン] single; simple

■ And the last kanji in this group is based on the shape of a flat fan. As a corollary to this thin and flat shape, it has come to signify the concepts of simple and only one.

■[簡単] easy, simple; [単語] word

241

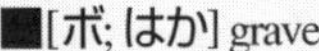

■[ボ; はか] grave

■The next three kanji all have three elements in common: the radical *kusakanmuri* [艹] on top, which is used in words related to plants, especially grasses and flowering plants; *hi* [日] in the middle, representing the sun; and the element [𠆢] below that, which also indicates grass. The overall picture created by these three elements [莫] is of grasses silhouetted against the setting sun, conveying the idea of dusk or twilight. Looking now at the first of these kanji, we see *tsuchi* [土], symbolizing soil or the ground, at the base. The resulting meaning, grave, is quite easy to infer—after the twilight of life comes death, when one's remains are buried in the earth.

■[墓地(ぼち)] graveyard, cemetery

242

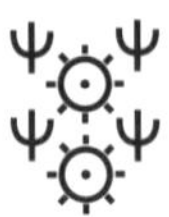

■[ボ; く(れる)] year end; to grow dark; to end; [くら(す)] to live, make a living

■The character *hi* [日] (sun) is both in the middle of this kanji and at the base, emphasizing the sun setting in the distance over a grass-covered plain. This signifies night falling, and also has meanings associated with ending or completion. The additional meanings, to live or to make a living, are derived from the idea of the sun setting on each day as it passes.

■[夕暮(ゆうぐ)れ] evening, twilight; [日暮里(にっぽり)] Nippori (district of Tokyo)

243

■[マク, バク] curtain, screen, hangings; act (of a play, etc.)

■The third kanji in this group has the character [巾] (cloth), at its base. The connotation here is the act of screening an area off with cloth to block out the sun or to hide something from view, and is derived from the practice, throughout history, of screening off certain areas in military encampments. This leads to such meanings as curtain, screen, hangings, and so on, as well as referring to the act of a play.

■[開幕(かいまく)] curtain raising, opening; [幕府(ばくふ)] shogunate

244

■[コウ; かま(える)] to build, set up; [かま(う)] to mind, care about

■The next pair of kanji both have the element [冓] on the right, symbolizing a wooden framework or structure. The first of these kanji has the radical *kihen*, signifying a tree, on the left. By putting these elements together, this character symbolizes the skillful building of a well-balanced wooden structure and so, by extension, means caring about something.

■[構造(こうぞう)] structure

245

■[コウ] lecture; club; study

■The second of this pair has *gonben* [言], related to words or speaking, as its left-hand radical. With the symbol for a framework or structure on the right, the core meaning becomes to make sentences from words so as to be understood. From this come such meanings as lecture, club, and study. Note that both kanji in this pair have the Chinese phonetical reading *kō*, but this one has no Japanese reading.

■[講義(こうぎ)] lecture; [講師(こうし)] lecturer, instructor

246

■[チャク, ジャク] arrival; clothing; [き(る), つ(ける)] to put on, wear; [き(せる)] to dress (someone); [つ(く)] to reach, arrive

■The upper element [𦍌] here is a modification of the character *hitsuji* [羊] (see No. 93), meaning sheep, while below is the character *me* [目], or eye. The meaning derived from these roots is quite humorous, if a little farfetched, with the idea of a sheep's wool hanging down over its eyes leading to the concept of being attached—perhaps from the idea of wool, attached to the head, hanging down in long strands. This, in turn, has evolved into two meanings: putting on or wearing clothes (think of 'attaching' them to one's body), and arriving somewhere (possibly a place to which one feels some attachment).

■[着物(きもの)] kimono, clothing; [到着(とうちゃく)] arrival

247

■[カン] to watch, see

■This time the upper element [龵] symbolizes a hand, with the character for eye again in the lower position. For once, the meaning is fairly logical: shielding one's eyes with one's hand to block out the sun or focus one's attention, in order to see clearly or to watch over something.

■[看護婦(かんごふ)] nurse

248

■[リ] traditional unit of distance (about 4 km); [り; さと] village, country, hometown

■The next five kanji are unusual because, although composed of similar elements, each has a different origin. The first has *ta* [田] (No. 157), representing a rice paddy, above *tsuchi* [土] (No. 50), meaning soil or ground. This signifies a rural village or farming community. Other meanings include hometown, and the *ri*, a traditional unit of distance that is no longer used.

■[村里(むらざと)] village

249

■[コク; くろ, くろ(い)] black

■Rather than depicting a rice paddy, the character [田] in this kanji is modeled after the top of a chimney, while the lower part [灬] symbolizes flames. The idea here is that a chimney becomes coated with soot, giving us the meaning black.

■[黒髪(くろかみ)] black hair

250

■[ギョ; うお, さかな] fish

■This character is modeled after the shape of a fish. You will find this character functioning as the left-hand radical in the names of several fish on the menu at your local sushi shop.

■[魚屋(さかなや)] fish shop; [鮮魚(せんぎょ)] fresh fish

251

■[ジュウ, チョウ; おも(い)] heavy; [かさ(ねる)] to pile up; [かさ(なる)] to be piled up; [え] -fold

■The fourth kanji in this group depicts a person standing on the ground holding a load. The size of the load implies that it is rather weighty, leading to the core meaning, heavy, and by extension, to pile up or to accumulate.

■[体重(たいじゅう)] one's body weight; [貴重品(きちょうひん)] article of value, valuables

252

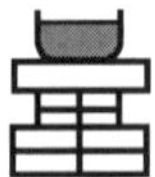

■[リョウ] quantity; [はか(る)] to measure, weigh

■And the final kanji in this group represents a rather heavy-looking stack of various items with a container of grain on top. This signifies measuring the weight, size, or quantity of things, as well as the concept of quantity itself.

■[大量(たいりょう)] a large quantity; [雨量(うりょう)] rainfall

253

■[セイ] fine weather; [は(れる)] to clear up; to be dispelled; [は(らす)] to clear (something) up

■Now we have a group of four kanji, all with the character *ao* [青], meaning blue, on the right. The first of these has the radical *hihen* [日], representing the sun, on the left. When the sun is out and the sky is blue, the weather must be fine.

■[秋晴(あきば)れ] fine autumn weather

254

清

■[セイ, ショウ; きよ(い)] pure, clear; [きよ(まる)] to become pure; [きよ(める)] to purify

■On the left this time is the radical *sanzui* [氵], signifying water. The concept of water, in combination with the color blue, symbolizes something that is pure and clear.

■[清流(せいりゅう)] clear stream

255

精

■[セイ, ショウ] spirit, energy, vitality; preciseness

■The third kanji in this group has the radical *komehen* [米], meaning rice, on the left. With the character for blue, signifying transparency or purity, on the right, we have the idea of somebody patiently cleaning or polishing rice to make it ready for eating. By extension, this kanji is associated with such concepts as energy or vitality, putting one's heart into something, and excellence.

■[精神(せいしん)] spirit, mind, soul; [精力(せいりょく)] energy, vitality

256

情

■[ジョウ, セイ] feeling(s), emotion, sympathy, circumstances; [なさ(け)] sympathy

■And the final kanji of this series has the radical *risshinben* [忄], meaning heart, in the spiritual or emotional sense, on the left. With the character for blue again on the right, we have the concept of a pure heart, leading to such meanings as sincerity, sympathy, consideration for others, and so on.

■[同情(どうじょう)] sympathy, compassion; [事情(じじょう)] circumstances, situation

257

明

■[メイ] light; [ミョウ] light; next; [あ(かり)] light, clearness; [あか(るい)] bright; [あか(るむ), あか(らむ), あ(ける)] to dawn; [あき(らか)] clear; [あ(く)] to be open; [あ(くる)] next; [あ(かす)] to pass (the night); to reveal

■The next pair of kanji have the radical *hihen* [日], symbolizing the sun, on the left, but are opposite in meaning. In the first of these, the character *tsuki* [月], meaning moon, is on the right. The sun and moon illuminate the day and night, giving rise to the core meanings: light and bright. An easy way to memorize this kanji is to remember that if the sun and moon are lined up side by side, it must be bright.

■[夜(よ)明(あ)け] dawn, daybreak

258

■[アン; くら(い)] dark, dim

■The character on the right this time is *oto* [音], meaning sound. The implication here is that the sun has set and only sounds can be detected in the darkness.

■[まっ暗(くら)] pitch dark; [暗記(あんき)] memorization

259

晩

■[バン] evening, night

■ Now we have a pair of kanji containing the character [免], which signifies to escape, to be exempted, or to get out of a situation. (The origins of this character are quite complex, and not very useful when trying to remember its meaning. As a memory aid you could picture it as someone running away, with [⺈] representing the head and body and [儿] the legs.) In the first of this pair, [免] is on the right, with the radical *hihen* [日], symbolizing the sun, on the left. This signifies that one is free from work once the sun has set; that is, when evening or night falls.

こんばん
■[今晩] this evening, tonight

260

■[ベン] hard work; to make efforts

■ When the radical *chikara* [力] (see No. 23), symbolizing power or strength, is placed on the right, with the character [免] on the left, the meaning becomes to focus one's energies on a task in order to be free of it. This will probably remind many readers of their efforts to study Japanese!

べんきょう
■[勉強] study

261

現

■[ゲン] the present; [あらわ(れる)] to appear, come in sight; [あらわ(す)] to show, reveal

■The radical on the left in the next two kanji is *ōhen* [⺩] (see No. 116), meaning king. In the first of this pair, the right-hand element is *mi(ru)* [見] (No. 7), meaning to see. The king is seen; he appears in front of his subjects. Hence the general meanings to appear or reveal, and the idea of something being before one's eyes, and therefore existing in the present.

■[現代(げんだい)] the present day, modern times

262

理

■[リ] logic, reason, principle

■The right-hand character this time is *sato* [里] (see No. 248), meaning village or rural community. The king marks out the land systematically, and villages are born. From this come such meanings as logic, reason, principle, and so on.

■[理由(りゆう)] reason, cause; [理論(りろん)] theory

263

朝

■[チョウ; あさ] morning; dynasty

■Next we have a group of four kanji, all of which have the character *tsuki* [月], meaning moon, on the right. (See No. 330 for more information on *tsuki.*) In the first of these kanji, the left-hand element [𠦝] represents the rising sun, seen through stalks of grass. The implication here is that at daybreak the rising sun takes the place of the moon. This kanji also means dynasty.

■[朝日(あさひ)] the morning sun; [平安朝(へいあんちょう)] the Heian Period

264

期

■[キ, ゴ] period, term

■ On the left this time is the element [其], depicting a square bamboo basket used to sieve cereals, and a square stand or base. This conveys the idea of things being neat and orderly. With the addition of the moon, which regularly waxes and wanes, the meaning becomes a fixed period or term.

■[期間(きかん)] period of time, term; [学期(がっき)] school term, semester

265

■[コ; みずうみ] lake

■ In the third kanji of this series the radical *sanzui* [氵], meaning water, is on the left and *furu(i)* [古], meaning old, is in the middle. With the character for moon again on the right, we find ourselves in a place where the moon is reflected in a body of 'old' water. 'Old' in this case has two nuances: the still water of a lake as opposed to the fresh, flowing water of a river, and the idea of a lake existing since time immemorial.

■[火口湖(かこうこ)] crater lake; [山中湖(やまなかこ)] Lake Yamanaka

266

■[チョウ; しお] tide; seawater; opportunity

■ And the last kanji in this quartet has *sanzui* [氵] (water) on the left, together with *asa* [朝], the first character of this group, meaning morning. This combination expresses the phenomenon of the morning tide, and by extension, tides and seawater in general. As a further corollary, this kanji also implies opportunity, reflecting the idea of a favorable tide.

■[満潮(まんちょう)] high tide; [干潮(かんちょう)] low tide

267

■[デン] electricity

■The following five kanji are often confused with each other, since the main element of each is the character *ame* [雨], meaning rain. In the first of these, rain is on top (as the radical *amekanmuri*) and [电], signifying lightning, is underneath. A rainstorm with lightning flashing across the sky represents the most primal form of electricity; hence the meaning of this kanji.

■[電気料金(でんきりょうきん)] electricity charges; [電話(でんわ)] telephone

268

■[セツ; ゆき] snow

■Again we have a kanji with *amekanmuri* on top. The character that once constituted the base of this kanji is no longer in use, but its meaning was associated with a broom or with sweeping things clean. Nowadays, this has been replaced by the katakana character *yo* [ヨ] but the former significance remains—snow falling like rain, 'sweeping' the landscape clean with its mantle of white. Picturing [ヨ] as the bristles of a broom might be a convenient way to remember the meaning of this kanji, if you can associate this in your mind with the scene of a fresh snowfall.

■[雪国(ゆきぐに)] snow country

269

■[ライ;かみなり] thunder, lightning

■This kanji originally consisted of the character for rain on top of three small circular marks (see diagram) which signified drums. Over the course of time the small circles have evolved into the character [田], but the overall connotation remains the same: the booming sound of a thunderstorm, like drums in the sky. Note that *kaminari* can mean thunder or lightning.

■[雷雨(らいう)] a thunderstorm

270

■[ウン; くも] cloud

■The element [云] was originally used by itself to signify clouds and, although *amekanmuri* was later added on top, the meaning remains the same. (Needless to say, the association of rain with clouds is perfectly logical.)

■[雲海(うんかい)] a sea of clouds; [夕焼雲(ゆうやけぐも)] sunset clouds

271

■[ドン; くも(る)] cloudy; to become cloudy, fogged

■The last member of this group consists of the preceding kanji, *kumo* [雲], surmounted by the character *hi* [日], which represents the sun. This conveys the image of a cloud blocking the sun, resulting in overcast or cloudy weather and, by extension, the idea of windows or spectacles becoming fogged by condensation.

■[曇(くも)り空(ぞら)] cloudy sky

272

■[シュ; さけ, さか] sake, rice wine, liquor

■ The left-hand radical here is *sanzui* [氵], representing water, while the character [酉], on the right, is shaped like a jar or container. This combination gives the kanji for sake, which has come to include other alcoholic drinks as well.

■[酒屋(さかや)] liquor store, sake dealer; [居酒屋(いざかや)] pub, tavern

273

■[ハイ, パイ; くば(る)] to distribute, deliver

■ The sake container is on the left this time, with the figure of a person kneeling down on the right. A person kneels beside a sake container to dole the precious liquid out to others, from which come the meanings to distribute or to deliver.

■[配達(はいたつ)] delivery; [心配(しんぱい)] worry, concern

274

■[ハン; めし] cooked rice, meal, food

■ The next two kanji have the radical *shokuhen* [飠], a modified form of *ta(beru)* [食] (to eat), on the left. In the first of these, [反] on the right represents a hand pressing a thin board so as to to warp it (see No. 59). No matter how many times the board is pressed, once the pressure is released it springs back to its normal shape. In combination with *shokuhen*, we get a character that means rice, or any food that is eaten every day.

■[朝御飯(あさごはん)] breakfast

275

■[イン; の(む)] to drink

■This time, the element [欠] on the right depicts a person opening their mouth wide, although this is one of those times when you'll have to use your imagination. In conjunction with *shokuhen*, this kanji conveys the act of opening one's mouth to swallow something down—in other words, to drink—as opposed to eating food as represented by *meshi* [飯] above.

■[飲酒(いんしゅ)] drinking (of alcoholic beverages)

276

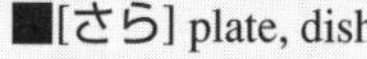

■[さら] plate, dish

■ This kanji, in the shape of a serving plate or dish, is nice and simple. The character *sara* is used as a radical in the lower position of various characters to indicate the basic shape of a container, for example in the word *bon* [盆], meaning tray.

■[灰皿(はいざら)] ashtray

277

■[ケツ;ち] blood

■ The addition of a diagonal stroke [ノ] to *sara*, described above, changes the meaning drastically, from an innocuous plate to a chalice containing the blood of an animal sacrificed to a deity. Hence the meaning: blood.

■[血圧(けつあつ)] blood pressure

278

■[シャ; もの] person

■ This kanji was originally derived from the image of a stack of firewood burning on a cooking stove. Subsequently it came to mean person, although the process by which this occurred is somewhat convoluted. At any rate, thinking of a person cooking over a wood stove might be a useful memory aid.

■[医者(いしゃ)] doctor; [悪者(わるもの)] rogue, rascal, scoundrel

279

■[ショ; あつ(い)] hot (weather)

■ The next two kanji are both formed with the preceding kanji, *mono* [者], as a major element. In the first, *mono* appears in the lower position to imply firewood burning on a stove, and this is surmounted by the character *hi* [日] (sun) on top. A burning stove combined with the heat of the sun—whoever created this kanji made doubly sure that the meaning 'hot' would be understood! Note that the word *atsui* formed with this kanji is only used in reference to atmospheric temperature, as indicated by the sun in the top position. (See also *atsu(i)* [熱], No. 388.)

■[むし暑(あつ)い] humid, muggy

280

■[ショ] station (police, fire, etc.); government office

■Again *mono* forms the base of this kanji, but this time it means a person. On top this time is [罒], depicting a net, which here signifies the act of squeezing things into a small enclosed space. Together they denote a government office, where people are packed into one place to work.

■[消防署(しょうぼうしょ)] fire station; [署名(しょめい)] signature, autograph

281

■[シュ; と(る)] to take, obtain

■Here the left-hand radical is *mimihen* [耳], based on an ear, while the element on the right depicts the shape of the right hand viewed from the side. In the distant past, soldiers in China would cut the ears off enemies they had slain in battle as proof that they had killed them. These rather gruesome roots should help to evoke the core meaning of this kanji: to take.

■[取材(しゅざい)] gathering of (news) materials, news coverage; [取引(とりひき)] business dealing, transaction

282

■[シュウ; おさ(める)] to obtain; to put away, put back; [おさ(まる)] to fit; to be restored

■Here, the element on the left represents two lengths of twine twisted together, signifying the act of putting things together. With the addition of a hand on the right, the meaning becomes to obtain something by gathering disconnected elements into a whole and, by extension, to put things away or back where they belong.

■[収入(しゅうにゅう)] income, revenue; [収集(しゅうしゅう)] collection, gathering

283

■[シ; うじ] family name; lineage

■ Here we have a fairly evocative image: an old house leaning to one side after many years of service, sheltering numerous generations. Despite this core suggestion of decline, as though the antiquated structure is about to fall over, this kanji in fact has a positive significance as it indicates the social standing of a family with a long lineage. When written after a person's name, the honorific *-shi* serves the same purpose as *-san* but with greater formality. If you have to fill out an official form, you will often find the word *shimei* (see below) indicating where you should write your name. (See also *seimei*, No. 302.)

■[氏名(しめい)] full name; [田中氏(たなかし)] Mr. Tanaka

284

■[ミン; たみ] people, subjects

■ This kanji also has quite graphic roots, depicting an eye in which the iris has been damaged or destroyed by a needle. This unfortunate combination originally signified a blind person, but later the meaning was broadened to encompass all people who blindly follow a ruler or leader, that is, the subjects of a country or a ruler. Nothing much seems to have changed since olden times—politicians still go to great lengths to ensure that the public sees as little as possible of what goes on behind the scenes.

■[国民(こくみん)] the people, nation; [民芸品(みんげいひん)] folk art, handicrafts

285

眼

■[ガン, ゲン; まなこ] eye

■ Now we come to a pair of kanji which both have the radical *mehen* [目] on the left, showing that they have some relationship to the eyes. In the first of these, the element on the right is [艮], signifying a person facing away from the sun. This combination conveys the idea of looking at something intently—think of keeping the sun behind you, illuminating the page, as you read a book. In contrast, the character *me* [目] (see No. 4) is simply based on the shape of the eye.

■[大田眼科(おおたがんか)] Dr. Ohta, Ophthalmologist (e.g., sign outside clinic)

286

■[ミン] sleep; [ねむ(る)] to sleep; [ねむ(い)] sleepy

■ In the second of this pair, the character [民] on the right is the *min* of *kokumin* [国民] (see No. 284), meaning a people or nation. As noted earlier in connection with this character, it was derived from the concept of people being blindly controlled or governed. When combined with *mehen* on the left, its meaning becomes a state in which the eyes cannot see; not blindness, but sleep.

■[睡眠(すいみん)] sleep

287

直

■[チョク, ジキ] honest, direct; [ただ(ちに)] immediately; [なお(す)] to mend, correct, set right; [なお(る)] to be fixed

■The character *choku*, which forms a major part of the next four kanji, consists of three parts: [十] (signifying the number 10), [目] (eye), and [乚] (corner). If ten separate people look at something, every detail will be judged in a fair and square way. This leads to meanings related to things being straight or direct, as well as to correct or to set something right.

■[直接(ちょくせつ)] direct; [正直(しょうじき)] honesty

288

■[チ; お(く)] to put, to place

■ With the addition of [罒], representing a net, on top of *choku*, we have the concept of setting a net in a straight line. The corollary of this is to place something in position or to set up something.

■[置(お)き物(もの)] ornament; [配置(はいち)] arrangement, stationing

289

■[ショク; う(える)] to plant; to set (type); [う(わる)] to be planted

■ This time, the radical *kihen* [木], meaning tree, is added to the left of *choku*. This signifies to make a tree stand up straight or, in other words, to plant something.

■[植物(しょくぶつ)] plant, vegetation

290

値

■[チ; あたい] value; [ね, あたい] price

■ And when the left-hand radical is *ninben* [亻], meaning person, the meaning changes to the value of a thing as determined by the judgment of many people's eyes.

■[値段(ねだん)] price; [価値(かち)] value, worth

291

■[イ; かこ(む), かこ(う)] to surround, enclose, encircle, lay siege to

■ Now we come to a group of five kanji which are all characterized by the radical *kunigamae* [口], representing an enclosure. The first of these kanji has the element [井] in the middle, depicting a well. From the image of a well bordered by some form of enclosure—possibly a low stone wall—comes the core meaning: to surround or enclose something.

■[周囲(しゅうい)] circumference; surroundings

292

■[ズ] drawing, diagram, plan; [ト; はか(る)] to plan, devise

■ The second kanji symbolizes a map of a geographical area, drawn within an enclosing perimeter. From this come such associated concepts as drawings, diagrams and plans, as well as planning or devising things.

■[地図(ちず)] map; [図書館(としょかん)] library

293

■[ダン, トン] group, association; suffix for troupe or company

■The inner element [寸] of this kanji symbolizes a hand curled into a circular shape. When combined with enclosure, the core meaning becomes to envelop things in a circle, leading to extended meanings such as gathering together, group, association, and so on.

■[団体(だんたい)] group, organization; [楽団(がくだん)] orchestra, band

294

■[コン; こま(る)] to be troubled, have difficulty

■Be careful of the fourth and fifth kanji in this group: they are quite similar in appearance but their meanings are totally different. The inner element [木] here is, of course, a tree. A tree in an enclosure will have problems growing, due to the limited space available for it to spread its roots and branches. Hence the connotations of being troubled or having difficulty.

■[困難(こんなん)] difficulty, trouble, sufferings

295

■[イン] cause; [よ(る)] to be based on, due to

■This time the enclosure represents a futon, on which is the character *dai* [大] (see No. 14), looking like a person with arms and legs outstretched. Thus the overall image is someone lying on a futon. And, just as a futon serves as a secure 'base' for a good night's sleep, this kanji means to be based on or to be due to something, as well as meaning cause.

■[原因(げんいん)] cause, factor, origin

296

■[オン] kindness, favor

■Next we have a trio of kanji with the radical *kokoro* [心], symbolizing the heart, in the lower position. The upper element of the first member is, of course, the preceding kanji, *in* [因]. Combined with the radical for heart underneath, the implication is that a person gains a sense of security by relying on the goodness of others. From this come such meanings as kindness, receiving a favor or sympathy, and so on.

■[恩人(おんじん)] benefactor

297

■[シ; おも(う)] to think, believe

■In the second member of this group, the upper element is actually a modified version of a character that originally signified the brain. The meaning of this kanji is thus derived from the fact that the brain and the heart govern our thoughts and beliefs.

■[思(おも)い出(で)] memories, recollections

298

■[ソク; いき] breath

■The upper element of the third kanji is modeled on the shape of the nose (see No. 5). The meaning of this combination becomes clear when you learn that, in the past, people thought that the breath originated in the heart before coming out through the nose.

■[休息(きゅうそく)] rest, relaxation

299

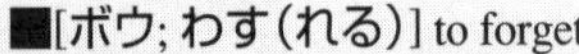

■[ボウ; わす(れる)] to forget

■ The following pair of kanji also contain the radical for heart, but in different positions. In the first of these, *kokoro* is again on the bottom as in the previous group, while this time the upper element [亡] signifies a person hiding or disappearing. This combination indicates things disappearing from the heart or mind, or in other words, forgetting.

■[忘年会(ぼうねんかい)] year-end party

300

■[ボウ; いそが(しい)] busy

■ This time the representation for heart appears as the radical *risshinben* [忄] on the left, while the right-hand element [亡] is the same as the one we saw on top in the preceding kanji, meaning to disappear. What this implies, in essence, is the same meaning as the preceding kanji, *wasu(reru)*, with the added nuance that one is so busy as to have become forgetful. To distinguish this kanji from its very similar cousin, you might like to imagine that the elements forming *isoga(shii)* are side by side, just as the tasks of a busy person follow one after another in quick succession.

■[多忙(たぼう)] the state of being busy, having much to do

301

性

■[セイ] sex; nature; [ショウ] temperament

■Now we come to a pair of kanji which are not only similar in appearance, but which have exactly the same pronunciation. Needless to say, their meanings are entirely different. In the first, the radical on the left is *risshinben* [忄], meaning heart in the spiritual or emotional sense, while on the right is the character *u(mareru)* [生] (see No. 77), meaning to be born. This combination denotes the nature or temperament that one has from birth and, by extension, sex or gender.

■[性質(せいしつ)] nature, property; [男性(だんせい)] male, man

302

■[セイ, ショウ] surname, family name

■This time the radical *onnahen* [女], meaning woman, is on the left and *u(mareru)* appears again on the right. Signified here is a person's name being passed down from mother to daughter, reflecting the matrilineal nature of both Chinese and Japanese society in olden times. You will often find the word *seimei* (see below) on official forms indicating the space where you should fill in your name. The difference between this word and *shimei* [氏名] (see No. 283) is that *seimei* is often divided into two boxes on a form, *sei* [姓] indicating the space for writing your family name and *mei* [名] the space for your given name(s).

■[姓名(せいめい)] full name

303

■[ジュ; う(ける)] to receive; [う(かる)] to pass (an examination)

■This kanji combines [⺤] and [又] both of which signify the shape of a hand, with [冖] in the middle symbolizing something to be handed over. This gives its overall meaning, receiving something from hand to hand, and by extension, passing an examination.

■[受験(じゅけん)] sitting an examination; [受身(うけみ)] passivity; passive voice (in grammar)

304

■[アイ] love

■In line with the description for the preceding kanji, the combination [爫] signifies handing over or giving something. With [夂] at the bottom, symbolizing legs, and *kokoro* [心], or heart, in between, we have the concepts of giving from the heart and acting out of a spirit of generosity or compassion (with the concept of action represented by the legs)—in a word, love. All of this is rather complicated, but if you think of *kokoro* in the central position you will probably be able to remember the other elements.

■[愛情(あいじょう)] love, affection (more general sense); [恋愛(れんあい)] love, romance (between a couple)

305

■[レン; こい] (romantic) love; [こ(う)] to be in love, long for; [こい(しい)] dear, beloved

■Here we have another kanji that means love. This time *kokoro* forms the base, while the upper element is a simplification of the character [戀] which used to appear in this position. This is a combination of [糸] (thread) on both left and right, with [言] (speaking or words) sandwiched in between, signifying a love in which it is impossible to express one's feelings because one is so enmeshed in the bonds ('threads') of endearment. To remember the current upper element, you may find it convenient to note that it consists of [亠] as in [言], the lower two strokes [丿|] as in the left-hand [糸], and the lower two strokes [丨丶] as in the right-hand [糸], respectively. Take care if you're writing a love letter not to mistakenly use the next kanji, which has the element signifying legs at the base, otherwise instead of saying *koishii* (I long for you) you might accidentally say *henshii*, which isn't a real word!

■[恋人(こいびと)] one's boyfriend/girlfriend, lover

306

■[ヘン] strange, odd; change; [か(わる)] to change, be altered; [か(える)] to change something

■As noted above, when the element [夂], symbolizing legs, replaces *kokoro* in the lower position, a completely different meaning results; namely, the idea of legs becoming entangled. This leads to the concept of something going wrong or being strange, and by extension, means change or alteration.

■[大変(たいへん)] very; difficult; serious; [変化(へんか)] change, variation

307

■[シ; わたくし] I; private

■The next pair of kanji both have the radical *nogihen* [禾] on the left, which signifies an ear of rice or some other cereal. In the first of these kanji, the right-hand element [ム] represents holding something in the crook of one's arm. From the concept of carrying ears of grain from the fields in one's arms (thus taking possession of them) comes the meaning I or oneself.

■[私立大学（しりつだいがく）] private university

308

■[ワ, オ] harmony, peace; [やわ(らぐ); なご(む)] to be softened, calm down; [やわ(らげる)] to soften (something); [なご(やか)] mild, peaceful, harmonious

■The second kanji of this pair has the character *kuchi* [口], meaning mouth, on the right. What does the combination of an ear of rice and a mouth signify? When people are well fed, disputes are less likely to occur and goodwill reigns. Thus we have such meanings as harmony, peace, and to be softened.

■[平和（へいわ）] peace

309

■[ミ; あじ] taste; [あじ(わう)] to taste; to appreciate

■The next two kanji have the character *mi* [未] (see No. 98) as their right-hand element, which means not yet in each case. The first of these has the radical *kuchihen* [口], symbolizing a mouth, on the left, signifying something one has not yet eaten, and therefore has not yet tasted. This, in turn, leads to the meaning to taste, as well as taste in itself.

■[甘味（あまみ）] sweetness; [趣味（しゅみ）] hobby; taste (in clothes, etc.); [興味（きょうみ）] interest

310

妹

■[マイ; いもうと] younger sister

■ When the radical *onnahen* [女] is placed on the left, the connotation becomes a female who has not yet become mature; a younger woman. This has come to mean younger sister.

■[姉妹 (しまい)] sisters

311

■[むすめ] girl, daughter

■ The next three kanji also have the radical *onnahen* [女], meaning woman, on the left. On the right of the first kanji is the character *yo(i)* [良], meaning good. The idea conveyed here is that a young girl is the epitome of a 'good woman.'

■[箱入り娘 (はこいりむすめ)] (lit., 'girl in a box') a well-protected daughter

312

■[コン] marriage

■On the right is [氏] (see No. 283) on top, depicting a leaning shape with the implication of decline or falling, and below is *hi* [日], signifying the sun. This combination conveys the idea of evening, when the sun goes down. With *onnahen* on the left, these combined elements mean marriage. This is not to imply that marriage is the sunset of one's life, but reflects the fact that in ancient China marriage ceremonies were usually held at dusk.

■[結婚 (けっこん)] marriage, matrimony

313

■[カ] to marry (a man); to shift responsibility onto (someone else); [とつ(ぐ)] to get married; [よめ] bride; daughter-in-law

■Again we find *onnahen* on the left, with *ie* [家] (see No. 179), meaning house or family, on the right this time. This combination signifies a woman marrying into another family. From the traditional concept of a woman moving to another household upon marriage, this kanji has also become associated with the idea of shifting responsibility onto someone else.

■[花嫁(はなよめ)] bride; [転嫁(てんか)] imputation, shifting (of responsibility)

314

■[カ; かせ(ぐ)] to work, earn a living

■This kanji has *ie* on the right again, but the left-hand radical in this case is *nogihen* [禾], signifying an ear of rice or some other cereal. The implication here is quite plain: harvesting the crops and bringing them to the house or, more generally, working hard at one's job to earn a living.

■[出稼(でかせ)ぎ] working away from home, migrant work

315

■[キ; かえ(る)] to return; [かえ(す)] to allow to return, to dismiss

■The next pair have the same right-hand element: [帚] (a broom). The first kanji has [リ], a simplified version of an older, complex character, on the left. Think of this as depicting a road. Then, from the concept of sweeping the road outside one's house then going back indoors, you should be able to remember that this kanji means going back or returning.

■[帰国(きこく)] returning to one's country

316

■[フ] woman, wife

■This time the radical *onnahen* [女], meaning woman, is on the left. The depiction of a woman with a broom is all too clear — generally it refers to a grown woman and, by analogy, a wife.

■[夫婦] married couple; [婦人] lady, woman

317

■[キ] season

■The upper part [禾] of this kanji is derived from the shape of an ear of rice, below which is the character *ko* [子] (see No. 39), meaning child. A child represents the fruition of a seed and, combined with an ear of rice, the concept of a harvest is implied. By extension, this kanji has come to signify the seasons.

■[季節] season; [四季] the four seasons

318

■[イ] to entrust (with)

■Again we have the symbol for an ear of rice on top, but this time the lower character is *onna* [女], meaning woman. Just as ears of rice bend before the wind, women have traditionally followed men — remember, these kanji were developed in China and adopted in Japan many centuries ago! From this concept has come the meaning to entrust or leave something in the hands of someone else.

■[委員] committee member, delegate

319

■[ハン; さか] slope; hill

■ The next group of three kanji have the character *so(ru)* [反] (see No. 59) on the right, representing a hand pressing a thin board so as to warp it. The first of these kanji has the radical *tsuchihen* [扌], meaning soil or ground, on the left. 'Warped' land would be a fairly good definition of a slope, wouldn't you agree?

■[坂道] (さかみち) sloping road, slope

320

■[ハン; さか] slope; hill

■ The second member of this group is a bit of an anomaly. Instead of *tsuchihen*, the radical *kozatohen* [阝] (indicating a hill or mound formed by piles of earth) is on the left, but the core meanings and pronunciations of this kanji are identical to those of the preceding character. However, this kanji is only used in the name 'Osaka' and in a few words associated with that area.

■[大阪] (おおさか) Osaka; [阪神電鉄] (はんしんでんてつ) the Hanshin Dentetsu Line (connecting Osaka and Kobe)

321

■[ハン, バン; いた] board, plank

■ And the third kanji of this series has the radical *kihen* [木], signifying tree or wood, on the left. This combination reinforces its core meaning: a thin board or plank.

■[看板] (かんばん) signboard; [板戸] (いたど) wooden door

322

■[ジョウ; しろ] castle

■ Next we come to a pair of kanji with the radical *tsuchihen* [扌] (soil or ground) on the left, both of which have military origins. The right-hand element of the first kanji consists of the radical *hokogamae* [戈], representing a halberd (a type of lance), and *tei* [丁], which means either to pound something so as to make it firm or to hammer a nail into a flat surface. Together, these elements form the character *na(ru)* [成], which has various meanings including to become, to put together, and to complete. When *tsuchihen* is added, we get the overall concept of a castle built by erecting solid earthen walls.

■[松本城(まつもとじょう)] Matsumoto Castle (Nagano Prefecture); [城下町(じょうかまち)] castle town

323

■[イキ] boundary, border; region, area

■ The central element [口] here expresses the idea of a demarcated territory, protected by the symbol for a halberd [戈] which we saw in the preceding kanji. With *tsuchihen* on the left, we have the concept of soldiers bearing arms stationed on the borders of a country. Thus this character denotes a land boundary or a defined region or area.

■[地域(ちいき)] area, region, zone

324

腹

■[フク; はら] belly, abdomen; heart, mind

■Now we come to a group of three kanji, each with the same right-hand element. (In addition, all three have the same *on-yomi*, or Chinese phonetical reading: *fuku*.) This element consists of [⺈日] on top, representing a pile of objects, and [夂] underneath, which symbolizes a pair of legs but, in this context, also means being piled up. So what we have on the right is a doubly reinforced depiction of piling up or accumulation. Turning our attention to the left-hand element of the first member of this group, we find the radical *nikuzuki* [月], which is often seen in words associated with the body (see No. 330). Thus this kanji refers to the belly or abdomen, where the internal organs of the body are 'piled up' in the most complicated manner and, by extension, the heart or mind. If you need an additional hint to help you remember this kanji, think which part of the body is likely to pile up those unwanted kilograms as the years go by.

■[満腹(まんぷく)] full stomach

325

■[フク] to repeat; double; multiple

■The left-hand radical here is *koromohen* [衤], meaning clothes. When this is combined with the right-hand element, which means piling up or accumulation, we have the concept of layers of clothes, or clothes with linings. By extension, this kanji has become associated with the idea of repeating something two or more times, as well meaning complicated.

■[複雑(ふくざつ)] complexity, complication, intricacy

326

■[フク] re-, again; to return

■ On the left this time is the radical *gyōninben* [彳], which signifies travel along a path or road. In conjunction with the idea of piling up or accumulation, the implication becomes to retrace a path. This leads to the concepts of returning to an original or former state, and of repetition, which we also saw in the preceding kanji.

■[復習(ふくしゅう)] review, revision

327

■[ジョウ;ば] place

■ The next four kanji have the character [昜] on the right, signifying the sun rising high into the sky ([日] means sun, [彡] represents rays of sunlight, and [丂] symbolizes rising high). The first of these kanji has the radical *tsuchihen* [土], signifying soil or ground, on the left. This combination denotes an elevated piece of land illuminated by the sun, or simply a place or spot.

■[場所(ばしょ)] place, location; [会場(かいじょう)] meeting place, venue, site

328

■[トウ; ゆ] hot water

■ This time, the left-hand radical is *sanzui* [氵], signifying water. Water is warmed by the sun, leading to the meaning of this kanji: hot water.

■[銭湯(せんとう)] public bath

329

■[ヨウ] positive; male principle; sun

■Here, the radical on the left is *kozatohen* [阝], symbolizing a hill or mound formed by piles of earth. A hill is brightly illuminated by the sun; from this concept of brightness, the meanings positive and male ('yang') principle—as well as the sun itself—were subsequently derived.

■[太陽(たいよう)] the sun

330

■[チョウ] intestines

■In the last of these four kanji, the left-hand radical is *nikuzuki*. Watch out for the character *tsuki* [月] used as a radical. The radical *tsukihen* means moon, the core definition of this character, while *nikuzuki*, the radical used here, is derived from *niku* [肉], a simplification of *nikutai*, which means the human body. Although *tsukihen* and *nikuzuki* are identical in appearance [月], this radical is normally called *nikuzuki* in words associated with parts of the body. Now we have another slight complication: although the right-hand element [昜] looks the same as that in the preceding three kanji, here it is actually derived from completely different roots. At any rate, for the sake of convenience it may be useful to think of the human body combined with the shining sun. If you picture the rays of the sun stretching through the sky, this might help you to remember the intestines, which also extend for a long distance within the body.

■[胃腸(いちょう)] the stomach and intestines

331

街

■[ガイ, カイ; まち] street, avenue

■Each of the next two kanji consists of three parts, and the key to differentiating between them lies in the central element. Actually, the left and right elements comprise a single, enclosing-type radical called *gyōgamae*, which is formed from the character *i(ku)* [行], meaning to go or to come. Looking now at the central element of the first kanji, we see two *tsuchi* [土] characters—one on top of the other—representing earth piled on top of earth. This signifies a parcel of land, neatly bisected by a street or avenue, with people (and, nowadays, vehicles) busily coming and going. As an analogy, this kanji also means *machi* (town or city).

■[商店街 (しょうてんがい)] shopping street, shopping center

332

■[ジュツ] art; artifice, means

■The central part [朮] of the second kanji is modeled after an ear of *mochiawa*, a type of glutinous millet. This is a smaller cereal than rice and, from its association with small things, this kanji came to signify the small paths or lanes of a village which are used constantly by the local residents. As a further derivation, it then became connected with such concepts as usefulness, techniques or means, and the arts.

■[技術 (ぎじゅつ)] art, skill, technique, technology; [美術 (びじゅつ)] art, fine arts

333

階

■[カイ] story of a building, floor; grade

■The next three kanji all have *kozatohen* [阝] on the left, signifying a hill or mound formed by piles of earth. In the first kanji of this group, the upper right-hand element [比] depicts two people in a line, and below this is the character *shiro* [白] (white). *Shiro* actually originated from the character *hyaku* [百], meaning 100, but rather than indicating a color, here it signifies many people standing in line. (Note that the right-hand character [皆] by itself is *mina*, meaning all, everything, or everyone.) Combining this line of people with a mound of earth creates the concept of a flight of earthen stairs, producing such meanings as the stories or floors of a building, grades or ranks, and so on.

■[階段(かいだん)] stairs

334

陛

■[ヘイ] stairs of a palace

■The second kanji of this group is similar to the first one, *kai* [階]. The only difference is that the character [土] replaces [白] on the lower right. Once again, this symbolizes a flight of earthen stairs, but in this case the extended meaning is not the stories or floors of a building. Rather, this kanji is found only in the word *heika* [陛下], meaning '(Your) Majesty' as used in reference to an emperor or monarch. This is derived from the fact that, in the past, the stairs of the Emperor's palace were made of earth. To distinguish this kanji, it might be helpful to visualize the right-hand element [坒] here as the Emperor and Empress walking majestically along the ground.

■[天皇陛下(てんのうへいか)] His Majesty the Emperor

335

陸

■[リク] land

■This time, the right-hand element consists of the character *tsuchi* [土], signifying soil or ground, repeated above and below, while the two small strokes [ㇾ] in between represent the idea of spreading or stretching. Combined with *kozatohen* on the left, this kanji symbolizes an expanse of land that rises out of the ocean and stretches as far as the eye can see.

■[大陸(たいりく)] continent

336

■[ガン; きし] bank, shore, coast

■Now we come to a kanji with the character *yama* [山] on top, meaning mountain, and [厈] below, representing the exposed geological strata of a cliff. A mountain is eroded by an ocean or river, forming cliffs in which the strata of the earth can be seen. Hence the meanings: bank, shore, and coast.

■[沿岸(えんがん)] coast, shore

337

■[ガン; いわ] rock

■Again *yama* is on top, symbolizing a mountain, but this time the lower element is *ishi* [石], meaning stone. Think of chipping off a piece of a mountain — what you will have is, of course, a rock.

■[岩山(いわやま)] rocky mountain

338

■[サ, シャ; すな] sand

■ This time the character *ishi* [石] (which forms the radical *ishihen* in this position), meaning stone, is on the left, while on the right is the character *suko(shi)* [少] (see No. 13), meaning few or little. The connotation here is also quite clear: sand consists of small particles of stone.

■[砂漠 (さばく)] desert

339

■[ビョウ] second (unit of time, angle, latitude and longitude)

■ Here, the radical on the left is *nogihen* [禾], representing an ear of rice or some other cereal, and *suko(shi)* is again on the right. This combination denotes the smallest part of an ear of rice or some other cereal, namely the fine hairs extending from the seed pods (take a look next time you're in a farming area). From this comes the concept of the smallest unit of time, angular measurement, and geographical coordinates: the second.

■[三十秒 (さんじゅうびょう)] 30 seconds

340

■[ヘン; かえ(す)] to return something, give back; [かえ(る)] to return, go back

■Next we have a large group of kanji with the radical *shinnyō* [辶], meaning to travel along a path or road or to advance, on the left. (See also Nos. 147 and 149 to 153.) To begin with, let's look at a pair of kanji which share the *on-yomi* (Chinese phonetical reading): *hen*. The first of these has the character *so(ru)* [反] (see No. 59) on the right, signifying a hand pressing a thin board so as to warp it and, as a corollary, the concept of opposite or reverse. In combination with *shinnyō*, the connotation here is to travel in the opposite direction on the same road and, by extension, to return or give something back.

■[返事(へんじ)] answer, reply

341

■[ヘン, べ; あた(り)] vicinity

■On the right this time is the element [刀]. Although this looks identical to the character *katana*, meaning sword, it is really just a simplified form of a complex character that was previously used for this element. At any rate, it will be helpful to treat it as representing a sword here. If you think of cutting off a road with a sword as signifying an impasse or a place where a journey ends, and then imagine having to spend some time in the area as a result of such an impasse, the meaning of this kanji, vicinity, shouldn't be too hard to remember.

■[海辺(うみべ)] seashore; [この辺(へん)] in this neighborhood

342

■[レン] group; accompaniment; [つら(なる)] to stretch in a row; [つら(ねる)] to join, link, put in a row; [つ(れる)] to take along, be accompanied

■Now we come to a kanji that combines *shinnyō*, on the left, with *kuruma* [車], signifying a wheel or vehicle (see No. 133), on the right. From the idea of many vehicles driving past in succession come such meanings as to stretch in a row, to join, to link, to be accompanied, and so on.

■[連絡(れんらく)] connection, communication, contact

343

■[ウン] fate, luck; [ウン; はこ(ぶ)] to carry, transport

■This kanji is very similar to the preceding one, but here *kuruma* is surmounted by an enclosure [冖]. This creates the character *gun* [軍], which represents a group of soldiers surrounding a military vehicle (probably a chariot in times past); in other words, an army. The combination with *shinnyō* signifies an advancing army, carrying its weapons and food, and this has come to mean to carry or to transport.

■[運動(うんどう)] exercise; movement; [運転(うんてん)] driving

344

■[タツ] to arrive, reach, attain

■This time the right-hand character consists of *tsuchi* [土] (soil or ground), on top of *hitsuji* [羊] (sheep) (see No. 93). A sheep walks along a dirt track and reaches its destination; this gives rise to such meanings as to arrive, reach, attain, and so on.

■[発達(はったつ)] development, growth

345

進

■[シン; すす(む)] to progress; [すす(める)] to promote something

■ The radical [隹] on the right in this kanji represents a bird. The meaning to progress comes from the idea of traveling with the speed of a bird.

■[進歩(しんぽ)] progress, improvement

346

■[ソウ; おく(る)] to send

■ The right-hand character [关] here symbolizes holding something up with both hands. When combined with *shinnyō*, the meaning becomes to hold things and carry them somewhere; that is, to send.

■[送別会(そうべつかい)] farewell party; [郵送(ゆうそう)] mailing

347

■[ソク; はや(い), すみ(やか)] speedy, quick; [はや(める)] to quicken, speed something up

■ The character on the right this time is *taba* [束] (see No. 67), representing a bundle of wood. The implication of combining this with *shinnyō* is quite clever: rather than carrying pieces of wood separately, it is quicker to transport them in bundles.

■[速達(そくたつ)] express delivery (mail); [高速道路(こうそくどうろ)] expressway

348

遅

■[チ; おそ(い)] late; slow; [おく(れる)] to be late; [おく(らす)] to delay, defer

■ The right-hand element [犀] here is a modified form of *sai* [犀], meaning rhinoceros. The walk of a rhinoceros is slow—no wonder it's always late.

■[遅刻(ちこく)] late, behind time

349

退

■[タイ; しりぞ(く)] to retreat, retire; [しりぞ(ける)] to keep away, drive away

■ And the final kanji in this group has [艮] on the right, representing a person with their back to the sun. This combination signifies moving in the opposite direction to the sun, and thus is related to retreating or retiring. Note that the final pair of strokes [ㇾ] in the right-hand element differs slightly from the corresponding strokes [ㇾ] in the next two kanji, although the right-hand element itself is basically the same in each.

■[退職(たいしょく)] retirement, resignation; [退院(たいいん)] discharge from hospital

350

■[コン] root; perseverance; [ね] root, base

■ Continuing with the element [艮] on the right, we come to a kanji with the radical *kihen* [木], meaning tree, on the left. This combination signifies movement in the opposite direction to the upward-growing branches of a tree; that is, down toward the roots. Hence the concept of root, base, foundation, and so on.

■[根本(こんぽん)] basis; [根気(こんき)] perseverance, patience

351

■[ゲン; かぎ(る)] limit, to limit

■ On the left this time is the radical *kozatohen* [阝], representing a hill or mound formed from piles of earth. When one encounters a steep hill or cliff that blocks one's path, there is no choice but to retreat. This kanji is therefore used in expressions indicating a limit in terms of capability or time, and in situations where there is a strict limit as to what is permissible.

■[期限(きげん)] term, deadline; [制限(せいげん)] restriction, limit

352

■[トウ; な(げる)] to throw, abandon

■We now come to a group of four kanji with the radical *rumata* [殳] on the right, symbolizing a halberd, or spear, being held in the hand and, as a corollary, using a tool. In the first member of this group, the radical *tehen* [扌] is on the left, representing using the hand. The combination of holding a halberd and using one's hands leads, logically enough, to the concept of throwing something.

■[投手(とうしゅ)] (baseball) pitcher; [投票(とうひょう)] vote, ballot

353

■[サツ, サイ, セツ; ころ(す)] to kill

■In the second kanji of this group, the left-hand element has [メ] on top, meaning to bind, tie or harvest something, and [木] underneath, which is the character for tree, but here its extended meaning is plant or cereal. The concept of killing is derived from using a sharp tool to strip the branches off a tree or to harvest a grain like millet, and tying the branches or sheaves into bundles.

■[殺人(さつじん)] murder; [自殺(じさつ)] suicide

354

■[ヤク, エキ] office, duty, service; [エキ] war, service

■When the radical *gyōninben* [彳], signifying travel along a path or road, is placed on the left, we have the image of someone walking along holding a halberd or spear. Such a person will probably be someone who has the job of protecting the country, and from this come meanings associated with role, duty, and so on.

■[役人(やくにん)] government official; [役目(やくめ)] role, duty

355

■[ダン] step, degree, rank

■ And the final member of this quartet has the element [阝] on the left, representing a cliff with steps cut into it. From the combination of [阝] with the symbol for a halberd on the right, which signifies the edged tool used to form the steps, meanings such as step, degree and rank are derived.

■[空手三段(からてさんだん)] third *dan* in karate

356

■[ショウ; まね (く)] to invite, beckon; to cause

■ The next pair of kanji have the character [召] on the right, consisting of [刀] (sword) on top and [口] (mouth) beneath. This represents a lord instructing his page to bring his sword, and denotes having somebody come to one, or calling somebody to come. With the radical *tehen* [扌], which symbolizes using the hand, on the left, the meaning becomes to beckon or to invite.

■[招待(しょうたい)] invitation

357

■[ショウ] introduction

■ And with *itohen* [糸], meaning thread, as the left-hand radical, we have the image of calling two people together and connecting them as if by a thread. In other words, introducing them to each other.

■[紹介(しょうかい)] introduction, presentation

358

建

■[ケン, コン; たて(る)] to build; [た(つ)] to be built

■The meaning of this kanji is not so clear at first, but an understanding of its roots may make it clearer. The left-hand radical *ennyō* [廴] means to extend or advance in a certain direction (for example, along a road stretching into the distance), while [聿] on the right depicts a writing brush held upright in the hand. Together they signify a structure being erected — in other words, the process of building something.

■[建築家(けんちくか)] architect; [建物(たてもの)] a building

359

■[エン; の(べる), の(ばす)] to lengthen, prolong, postpone; [の(びる)] to be postponed, delayed, prolonged

■In this kanji, *ennyō* again appears on the left, but the character on the right here combines the symbol [止], representing feet or footprints, with a diagonal stroke [ノ] meaning to extend. The overall significance — which again is not so clear at first glance — is to prolong the duration of a journey by repeatedly stopping and starting.

■[ビザの延長(えんちょう)] visa extension; [延期(えんき)] postponement

360

■[ケン; すこ(やか)] healthy

■The third kanji in this group consists of *tate(ru)* [建] (No. 358), to build, with the radical *ninben* [亻], denoting a person, on the left. This expresses the idea that, just as a house is built, so too one builds up one's body. Thus the meaning strong or healthy is obtained.

■[健康(けんこう)] health, fitness; [健康保険証(けんこうほけんしょう)] health insurance card

361

■[テキ] fit for, suitable

■ Again we encounter the left-hand radical *shinnyō* [⻌] , meaning to travel along a path or road or to advance, while the element on the right — although a little complicated — signifies a drop of water falling from the roof with a plop. The concept of a falling drop of water, combined with the act of advancing step by step, has come to mean being fit or suitable. To help remember this, you could think of a drop of water adapting to the shape of the receptacle in which it lands, coupled with the idea of advancing or evolving into something more suitable than before.

■[適当(てきとう)] suitable, appropriate

362

■[テキ; かたき] enemy, opponent

■ This time the falling droplet is on the left, and the radical *nobun* [攵], representing a stick held in the hand, is on the right. Just as the drop of water falling from the roof will inevitably strike the ground, so two enemies confronting each other, weapons in hand, will come to blows. Note that this kanji has the same *on-yomi* (Chinese phonetical reading) as the preceding one: *teki*.

■[強敵(きょうてき)] powerful rival

363

■[ガン; かお] face

■Next is a group of kanji which have the radical *ōgai* [頁], signifying the head, on the right. (Note that the character *kubi* [首] (No. 6), meaning neck or head, has 'hair' [⺌] on top while *ōgai* has 'legs' [八] at the bottom.) In the first of these kanji, the three diagonal strokes [彡] on the lower left symbolize traditional hair ornaments such as women used to wear. The meaning contributed by the upper left part is a little complicated and not very helpful as a memory aid, but the overall connotation of this kanji is that the most beautiful part of the head is the face.

■[顔色(かおいろ)] (lit., 'color of the face') complexion, look, expression

364

■[トウ, ト, ズ; あたま, かしら] head; leader; top; brain

■Again the basic character signifying the head is on the right, but this time the left-hand element is the character *mame* [豆], meaning bean. This gives the most commonly used word for head, based on the notion that the head is shaped like a bean. Actually, *atama* usually refers to the top part of the head from the eyebrows up, and also has such related meanings as leader, top, and brain. To remember this kanji, it might help to think of the English colloquialism 'to bean someone,' meaning to strike someone on the head.

■[頭痛(ずつう)] headache; [頭(あたま)がいい] clever, brainy

365

■[ガン; ねが(う)] wish, petition, request; to wish, request

■This time the character on the left is *hara* [原] (see No. 195), meaning plain or field. When combined with *ōgai* on the right, we have the concept of a head—the seat of thoughts and desires—which is as large as a plain, giving the core meaning to wish or to request. As an aid to remembering this kanji, you could picture a broad expanse of fields encompassed by your own wishes and desires.

■[祈願(きがん)] prayer

366

■[ダイ] title, subject, theme

■The next kanji in this group has the element [是] on the left, combining the shape of a spoon with a long, straight handle above, and a leg underneath. This signifies advancing in a straight line. With the addition of [頁] *ōgai* again on the right, the overall connotation becomes the forehead—the 'straight' part of the head. And just as the forehead is at the front of the head, this kanji signifies the title, subject or theme which is positioned at the forefront of something. Sometimes these explanations may seem quite labyrinthine, but believe it or not they are generally agreed to be the actual roots of the kanji concerned.

■[問題(もんだい)] problem, issue, question

367

■[ヨ; あず(ける)] to entrust, deposit something with somebody; [あず(かる)] to keep, be entrusted, take care of
■This time we have the character *yo* [予] (see No. 40), meaning previously or in advance, on the left. Using one's head in advance means preparing for future eventualities, and the act of entrusting somebody with something is an extension of this. You will often see the word in the example below when you visit the bank.
■[預金(よきん)] deposit, savings

368

■[リョウ] governing, rule
■On the left here is [亽], meaning to gather, and below it is the representation of a person kneeling [マ]. This left-hand element has the connotation of ordering something to be done. When combined with *ōgai* on the right, which in this case has the implication of a person who gives orders (that is, someone who is at the head of things), the meaning becomes to govern or to rule, as well as referring to a person who rules.
■[大統領(だいとうりょう)] president (of a country); [領土(りょうど)] territory

369

■[ルイ] kind, type
■And the left-hand element of this kanji has *kome* [米] (rice) surmounting the image of a person with arms and legs outstretched [大]. Although it might seem farfetched at first, the combination of this element with *ōgai* conveys the idea that a grain of rice and the head or face of a person are similar in shape, thus symbolizing things that are associated or of the same type.
■[種類(しゅるい)] variety, type; [親類(しんるい)] a relative

370

■[スウ, ス; かず] number; [かぞ(える)] to count

■In this kanji, the character *kome* [米] (rice) at the upper left combined with *onna* [女] (woman) underneath signifies a row of women (think of a row of women in a paddy field, planting rice), while the radical *nōbun* [攵] at the right denotes a hand holding a rod. Taken together, these elements mean counting the number of women forming a line, and by extension, counting and numbers in general.

■[数字（すうじ）] numeral, digit; [数学（すうがく）] mathematics

371

■[タイ; か(す)] loan; to lend, rent out

■Now we come to a large group of kanji with the radical *kai* [貝] (see No. 8) at the base, which symbolizes a shell and, by extension, money. The first member of this group has the character *ka(waru)* [代] on top. Looking at the composition of this character first, you will notice *ninben* [亻] (person) on the left and the element [弋] on the right, representing a stake that marks a boundary. From the concept of posting guards at a boundary instead of stakes, we arrive at the core meaning of *ka(waru)*: to replace something or somebody with something or somebody else. And now we come to the meaning of the present kanji with *ka(waru)* on top and *kai* below: to provide money on behalf of someone who is unable to pay; in other words, to lend.

■[貸自転車（かしじてんしゃ）] rental bicycle

372

■[ボウ] to exchange, trade

■The upper element [卯] here represents someone trying to pry open a window with both hands, although you could be forgiven if you didn't realize that straight away. With the addition of *kai*, this character conveys the idea of trying to make a profit by prying something open, in order to have somebody buy or sell goods. This seems to accurately describe the tactics used in world trade, wouldn't you agree?

■[貿易(ぼうえき)] trade, commerce

373

■[ヒン, ビン; まず(しい)] poverty; poor

■The character on top this time is *wa(keru)* [分], to divide. This is made from [八], meaning to divide a thing into two, and *katana* [刀] (sword), which also signifies dividing something in two with a sword. In combination with *kai* underneath, this kanji represents dividing money and property so that each person gets less, thus making them poor.

■[貧乏(びんぼう)] poverty

374

■[カ] treasure, goods

■In the upper position this time is *ka* [化] (see No. 80), meaning to turn into or to take the form of something. Money can be converted into various goods, so this kanji refers to things of value, including money itself.

■[百貨店(ひゃっかてん)] department store; [通貨(つうか)] currency

375

■[チン] wages; rent; fee

■ The upper character here is *nin* [任], consisting of *ninben* [亻] (person) on the left and the element [壬] on the right, denoting someone carrying a load on their back. This expresses the idea of playing an important part, and thus signifies duty or work. When combined with *kai*, the meaning becomes money paid as remuneration for work. It is also used to mean the fee for renting something.

■[家賃(やちん)] house rent

376

■[シ] wealth, help, nature, resources, capital, funds

■ This time, the character in the upper position is *tsugi* [次], meaning next. The radicals forming this character are [冫] on the left, meaning two, and [欠] on the right, portraying a person opening their mouth to yawn. This indicates the attitude of taking things easy, implying that there's no need to be first—being next in line is OK. In combination with *kai*, we arrive at a viewpoint that people have held since ancient times: next in importance to life itself is money or assets. From this come meanings associated with capital, resources, and again, money.

■[資源(しげん)] resources

377

■[シツ] quality, substance; [シチ, チ] pawn, hostage

■The upper part [斦] of this kanji represents two axes side by side. In combination with *kai*, the connotation becomes something equivalent in value to two axes, leading to such meanings as contents, quality, and substance. To remember the additional meaning of this kanji, pawn or hostage, it might be helpful to think of a terrorist with an axe in each hand demanding money in return for releasing a hostage.

■[性質(せいしつ)] characteristic, nature; [人質(ひとじち)] hostage

378

■[ヒ; つい(やす)] to spend, waste; [つい(える)] to be wasted

■The upper element [弗] here symbolizes steam or vapor rising from a river. When this is juxtaposed with *kai*, the implication is that money disappears like water. Hence the meanings: to spend or to waste. Incidentally, notice how the upper element resembles a back-to-front dollar sign ($)—this might also be a helpful memory aid.

■[費用(ひよう)] expense, cost

379

■[サン] praise; agreement

■Take care with the next two kanji; their upper elements are the same but their lower elements are slightly different. Looking at the top part of the first one we see the element [兟], portraying two men side by side. Once again, *kai* is at the base, signifying money or something of value. The inference here is that one man is welcoming a visitor and appreciating the excellent gift he has brought. Hence the core meaning: to praise.

■[賛成(さんせい)] agreement, approval, support

380

■[タイ; か(える)] to replace, exchange; [か(わる)] to take the place of

■ Instead of *kai*, the lower element here is [曰]. Be careful — this is not the character *hi* [日] but a wider character with a different meaning: words coming out of the mouth. Combining this with the upper element [夫夫] signifying two men side by side, we have two men talking to each other in order to change positions or swap tasks.

■[両替(りょうがえ)] money changing; [振替(ふりかえ)] transfer

381

■[キ; たっと(い), とうと(い)] valuable, noble; [たっと(ぶ), とうと(ぶ)] to value, respect

■ Returning to the group of kanji with *kai* in the lower position, the element [⾅] on top here denotes holding a large package or bundle with both hands. With *kai* signifying money, we have the connotation of conspicuous assets or property, and consequently, high value, as well as the associated concept of nobility.

■[貴重品(きちょうひん)] valuables; [貴族(きぞく)] a noble, the aristocracy

382

■[セキ; せ(める)] to condemn, blame, torture

■ And here we have the upper element [龶] depicting a branch of a tree with thorns at the tip. This combination signifies to press somebody to return money as if pricking them with thorns, leading to the extended meanings to condemn, blame, or torture.

■[責任(せきにん)] responsibility, obligation

383

積

■[セキ; つ(む)] to heap up, load; [つ(もる)] to be piled up

■The next two kanji have the character *se(meru)* [責] on the right, which, as we have just seen, has meanings including to condemn, to blame, and to torture. On the left is the radical *nogihen* [禾], representing an ear of rice or some other cereal. The meaning of this combination becomes clear when you remember that farmers were once tormented by taxes they had to pay in the form of rice, which was collected and stored in government warehouses. From this we get such meanings as to heap up, to be piled up, and so on.

■[積雪(せきせつ)] (fallen) snow; [面積(めんせき)] area, size

384

■[セキ] achievement; weaving

■This time, the left-hand radical is *itohen* [糸] (thread). When combined with *se(meru)*, again on the right, the meaning becomes to make cloth by continuously forcing thread together. (The idea of forcing is contributed by *se(meru)*; think of what a torturous process it must be for the thread!) This gives rise to the core meaning, weaving, as well as the achievement of a task or work.

■[成績(せいせき)] result, record, performance

385

■[ソク] law, rule; to act on (a principle)

■Next we come to three kanji that incorporate the character *kai* [貝], although not as a base. Apart from their physical similarity, note that all three have *soku* as their *on-yomi* (Chinese phonetical reading). In the first of these, *kai* is on the left as the radical *kaihen*, while the radical *rittō* [刂], depicting a sword, is on the right. The nuance here is to divide money or assets in a fair way, according to the appropriate laws and rules.

■[規則(きそく)] rule, regulation

386

■[ソク; はか(る)] to measure, fathom

■In the second member of this group, the radical *sanzui* [氵], symbolizing water, is added to the left of the preceding kanji. From the concept of measuring the depth of water according to a certain rule, this character derives its general meaning: measuring lengths, weights and so on.

■[測量(そくりょう)] survey; [予測(よそく)] estimate, forecast

387

■[ソク; かわ] side

■And in the third kanji, the left-hand radical is *ninben* [亻], signifying a person. This combination means side or proximity, due to the notion that people always keep rules by their side as a standard for action.

■[右側(みぎがわ)] right-hand side; [反対側(はんたいがわ)] opposite side

388

■[ネツ] heat; fever; zeal; [あつ(い)] hot (except weather)

■The next three kanji are slightly complex in terms of both structure and meaning, but there is a logic to it all. In the first member of this group, the character *maru* [丸] (see No. 26) on the upper right represents a person curled into a crouching position. Then, on the upper left, the character *tsuchi* [土] is repeated twice with two small strokes [ハ] in between, representing an expanse of soil or ground. The combination of these two elements symbolizes a person bending down and tilling the earth, or cultivating crops. With the four strokes [灬] at the bottom signifying a burning flame, the emphasis becomes the energy of a fire like the energy of vigorously growing crops. Note that this kanji is not used to refer to atmospheric temperature. (See also *atsu(i)* [暑], No. 279.)

■[熱心(ねっしん)] zeal, enthusiasm, eagerness

389

■[セイ; いきお(い)] force, energy, vigor

■This kanji is similar to the preceding one, except that the bottom character is *chikara* [力] (see No. 23), meaning force, power or strength. The more energy a farmer puts into cultivation, the stronger his crops will be. Thus such meanings as force, energy, vigor, momentum, influence, and so on are derived.

■[勢力(せいりょく)] influence, power, strength

390

■[ジュク; う(れる)] to ripen, mature

■The last kanji of this series is also similar to the first, but this time it is the upper left-hand element [享] that differs. The roots of this combination are somewhat obscure, but as a convenient device you could think of a child [子] being brought up in a warm and loving environment, leading to the meanings ripening or maturing well.

■[熟語(じゅくご)] idiomatic phrase; [熟睡(じゅくすい)] deep/sound sleep; [未熟(みじゅく)] unripe, immature

391

■[フツ; はら(う)] to pay; to sweep away, brush off

■The left-hand radical here is *tehen* [扌], which represents using the hand, while the character originally on the right signified pushing something troublesome away. For convenience, since the character on the right today looks like the katakana character *mu* [ム], think of brushing off something *muzukashii* (difficult) with the hand. This kanji also means to pay money to resolve a troublesome situation.

■[支払い(しはらい)] payment

392

■[ブツ; ほとけ] enlightened being; the Buddha

■With the radical *ninben* [亻], meaning person, on the left, and the same original character as in the last kanji (now changed to [ム]) on the right, we have a person who has transcended the trials and tribulations of this world. This kanji usually symbolizes the Buddha, although it is also used in connection with anyone who has attained enlightenment.

■[仏教(ぶっきょう)] Buddhism; [大仏(だいぶつ)] Great Buddha (statue)

393

制

■[セイ] system; regulations; to control

■ Here we have [𰀁] on the left, denoting a tree with protruding branches, while on the right is [刂] representing a sword or knife. This signifies trimming the branches of a tree to shape it, with the implication of putting things in order or systematizing them. Another meaning associated with this kanji is to make, particularly when things are individually crafted such as works of art. Take care not to confuse this meaning with the definition of manufacturing (i.e., mass production) of the following kanji, since both these kanji have the same reading (*sei*).

■[制度(せいど)] system; institution; [制限(せいげん)] restriction, limit

394

■[セイ] manufacture; make

■ When the character [衣], meaning clothing, is added as a lower element to the preceding kanji, we have the new definition of cutting cloth to make garments. This has been expanded to encompass making things in a general sense. But, as noted above, remember that this kanji is used when goods are mass produced rather than individually made.

■[電気製品(でんきせいひん)] electrical appliance; [日本製(にほんせい)] made in Japan

395

■[ケン] effect; to examine; [ゲン] effect, omen

■The next three kanji have [僉] on the right, consisting of [亼] (to gather), [口] (mouth), and [人] (person). Combined, these signify people gathering and discussing a topic to produce a particular viewpoint. Note that all three kanji in this group share the *on-yomi* (Chinese phonetical reading) *ken*. The first has the radical *umahen* [馬] (horse; see No. 104) on the left, and means to examine horses in order to select a good one.

■[試験(しけん)] examination, experiment, trial

396

■[ケン] to examine; inspection, investigation

■On the left this time is the radical *kihen* [木], meaning wood. When combined with the above-mentioned element, meaning to gather people's opinions, the image becomes one of collecting wooden tablets, each inscribed with different viewpoints or, in other words, inspection and investigation so as to preserve order.

■[検査(けんさ)] inspection, test, check

397

■[ケン; けわ(しい)] steep, fierce, severe

■And the third member of this group has the radical *kozatohen* [阝] on the left, signifying a hill or mound formed from piles of earth. To remember the meaning of this kanji, notice the perpendicular line that forms the left-hand side. When people gather together for a chat they all agree — this steep cliff is a dangerous place.

■[危険(きけん)] danger, risk

398

識

■[シキ] to know, discriminate

■The last three kanji have the element [戠] on the right. This consists of *oto* [音], meaning sound, and [戈], which is derived from the radical *shikigamae* [弋], meaning a sign or mark, but with the addition of a small extra stroke (which itself represents a mark) at the bottom. (Note that although it looks exactly the same, the character with the small extra stroke is not the radical *hokogamae* [戈], representing a halberd or spear.) The significance of this compound element thus becomes 'the signs of sounds,' or in other words, signs or marks that differentiate sounds from one another. And now we come to the first kanji in this group of three, which has the radical *gonben* [言], associated with words or speaking, on the left. The overall significance of this combination is to utter words as sounds with particular meanings, and as a corollary, to know things well or to discriminate between things.

■[知識(ちしき)] knowledge; [標識(ひょうしき)] sign, mark

399

■[ショク, シキ; お(る)] weaving; to weave

■The insertion of *itohen* [糸] (thread) as the left-hand radical signifies making a mark by tying threads together. From this combination the meaning of this kanji, binding threads together to weave a cloth with a loom, is derived.

■[織物(おりもの)] cloth, textile; [機織(はたお)り] weaving; a weaver

400

職

■[ショク] work, employment, position

■ And the final kanji in this trio has the radical *mimihen* [耳], meaning ear, on the left. This, of course, signifies distinguishing things by hearing characteristic sounds or signals. By extension, the meaning has become one's work or job, as something that one knows very well and can identify easily. Since these roots involve a rather large leap of logic, it may be helpful simply to remember that, in order to work, it is necessary to use one's ears to determine the needs and instructions of those around you.

■[職業(しょくぎょう)] job, occupation; [就職運動(しゅうしょくうんどう)] job hunting

EXERCISES

Test your knowledge by filling the blanks in the following sentences with the correct kanji. The sentences are arranged so that each contains two or more similar-looking kanji, and the various groups of kanji appear in approximately the same order as in the text.
To check your answers, see the answer key on page 189.

1. 十五(じゅうご)[　](にち)は三番(さんばん)[　](め)の弟(おとうと)(younger brother)のたんじょう[　](び)(birthday)ですから、[　](しろ)いシャツをプレゼントに買(か)いました。それは千九(せんきゅう)[　](ひゃく)円(えん)でした。

2. [　](じ)分(ぶん)のうちを出(で)て、[　](しゅ)都高速道路(とこうそくどうろ)(Metropolitan Expressway)を車(くるま)で走(はし)ります(run)。

3. デパートの[　](う)り場(ば)で、おいしそうな[　](かい)を[　](み)つけた(found)ので、それを[　](か)って、店(てん)[　](いん)(shop assistant)にお金(かね)をはらいました(paid)。

4. [てん]気(き)がいいので、[ふと]った人(ひと)は[おお]きい[いぬ]と[すこ]し[ちい]さい[いぬ]をつれて(taking along) さんぽしています(going for a walk)。
[いぬ]たちはとても[げん]気(き)です。

5. [みぎ]の[ほう]にある[うわ]着(ぎ)は二(に)[まん]円(えん)以(い)[じょう](more than)ですが、[ひだり]の[ほう]のは、二(に)[まん]円(えん)以(い)[か](less than)です。

6. [みぎ]にまがって(turn)[すこ]し行(い)くと、[ひだり]の[ほう]に博物館(はくぶつかん)(museum)があります。そこでは[ちから]の強(つよ)かった(powerful) 将軍(しょうぐん)(shogun)の[かたな]を見(み)ることができます。

7. あしたは[やす]みですから、[く]時(じ)からジム(gymnasium)で[たい]そう(exercises)をします。
[たい]そうがおわった[ひと]たちは、ジムの[いり]口(ぐち)にある[まる]いテーブルでお茶(ちゃ)をのんでいます。

8.　コンピューターの[　](つか)い[　](かた)(way of using)をおぼえれば仕事(しごと)をするのに[　](べん)利(り)です。

9.　[　](さく)日(じつ)はケーキを[　](つく)ったり、[　](て)紙(がみ)を書(か)いたりしました。今日(きょう)の[　](よ)定(てい)は、郵(ゆう)[　](びん)局(きょく)で[　](て)紙(がみ)を出(だ)してから、デパートへ[　](こ)どものジャケットと[　](もう)布(ふ)を買(か)いに行(い)きます。[　](け)糸(いと)のセーターも買(か)いたいです。そのデパートは郵(ゆう)[　](びん)局(きょく)から[　](みぎ)にまがって(turn)少(すこ)し行(い)くと、[　](ひだり)の方(ほう)にあります。

10.　[　](がく)生(せい)たちは、[　](がっ)校(こう)で、漢(かん)[　](じ)を習います(learn)。

11.　自(じ)[　](どう)車(しゃ)をつくる会社(かいしゃ)で[　](はたら)いています。

12.　[　](とく)別(べつ)に安(やす)く(cheap)なるまで[　](ま)って買(か)い[　](もの)をします。その[　](とき)は、大(おお)きなかばんを

[　]（も）って行（い）きます。

13. [　]（と）地（ち）を買（か）いたいので、弁護（べんご）[　]（し）とそうだんします(consult)。

14. わたくしは、会（かい）[　]（しゃ）で六時（ろくじ）まで[　]（し）事（ごと）をします。

15. [　]（はは）は[　]（まい）日（にち）、[　]（かい）岸（がん）のそばにある[　]（うめ）の木（き）のところまでジョギング(jogging)をしています。

16. 一人（ひとり）の[　]（とも）だちは[　]（いけ）袋駅（ぶくろえき）の[　]（ひがし）口（ぐち）にある[　]（こう）番（ばん）で働（はたら）いています。[　]（ほか）の[　]（とも）だちは[　]（はん）対（たい）の[　]（にし）口（ぐち）にある[　]（こう）番（ばん）で働（はたら）いています。[　]（ちち）は[　]（こう）番（ばん）のとなり(next door)にある大学（だいがく）で[　]（ぶん）学（がく）をおしえています。わたくしもその大学（だいがく）で勉強（べんきょう）していますから、時々（ときどき）、わたくしたちは[　]（ち）下鉄（かてつ）の入口（いりぐち）で会（あ）う約（やく）[　]（そく）をして、レストランへ行(い)きます。

17. [し]月(がつ)にさくらの[はな]がさきます(bloom)。[あめ]のふらない日(ひ)に[りょう]親(しん)(parents)といっしょに、[はな]見(み)に行(い)くつもりです。

18. わたくしたちのクラスは[せん][せい]と日(にっ)[こう]に行(い)きます。日(にっ)[こう]のガイドブックを一(いっ)[さつ]よむつもりです。みんなで[よん]十人(じゅうにん)ですから大(おお)きなバスを利(り)[よう]します。一人(ひとり)は5,000[えん]ぐらいはらいます(pay)。

19. わたしは駅(えき)の[きた]口(ぐち)にある大学(だいがく)で、[とう]洋(よう)(Oriental)の文(ぶん)[か](culture)と[せい]洋(よう)(Western)の文(ぶん)[か]の[りょう]方(ほう)を勉強(べんきょう)しています。文(ぶん)[か]のちがうところ(differences)を[くら]べるのはおもしろいです。

20. 国際(こくさい)[かい]議(ぎ)(international conference)があると、

[かっ]国(こく)の大統領(だいとうりょう)(president)の[な]前(まえ)がニュースに出(で)ます。

21. ABC英(えい)[かい]話学校(わがっこう)は入学(にゅうがく)するお[かね](school admission fee)とクラスのお[かね]と本(ほん)の[ぜん]部(ぶ)を[あわ]せても四万円(よんまんえん)です。

22. 五月中(ごがつちゅう)[じゅん]に俳(はい)[く]の会(かい)があります。

23. 両親(りょうしん)のぼくじょう(ranch)では、[うし]と[ひつじ]を[はん]分(ぶん)ずつ飼(か)っています(raising)。[らい]月(げつ)はぶた(pigs)も[く]るので、[ご]前(ぜん)も[ご]後(ご)もいそがしく(busy)なるでしょう。ふるさと(hometown)の[へい]野(や)は[うつく]しいので年(ねん)[まつ]には帰(かえ)りたいのですが、はっきりした(exact)ことは[み]定(てい)です。

24. 弓(ゆみ)(bow)のれんしゅうをはじめましたが、的(まと)(target)に[や]を射(い)る(shoot)のはむずかしく、

[　](しっ)敗(ぱい)ばかりです。

25. いなか(the countryside)の[　](みず)はおいしいですよ。雪(ゆき)や[　](こおり)がとけて(thaw)、地下(ちか)[　](すい)(subterranean water)になるのです。わたしはいなかに[　](えい)住(じゅう)したいですね。

26. [　](しま)ではたくさんの[　](とり)が飛(と)んでいます(flying)。ある[　](しま)には[　](うま)もいます。

27. 氷(ひょう)[　](が)時代(じだい)(the Ice Age)にも生物(せいぶつ)(living things)が住(す)むことが[　](か)能(のう)でした。

28. あなた方(がた)は[　](なん)時(じ)の電車(でんしゃ)で行(い)きますか。[　](おな)じホテルにとまる(stay)のですから、[　](む)こうで会(あ)いましょう。帰(かえ)りの切(きっ)[　](ぷ)は、わたしが持(も)っています。[　](に)物(もつ)は少(すこ)しにしましょうね。

29. 政(せい)[　](ふ)の人(ひと)たちは、大会社(だいがいしゃ)からの個人的(こじんてき)

(private) な寄（き）[　]（ふ）を受（う）けて(receive)はいけません。

30.　[　]（おう）女（じょ）(princess)様（さま）はたくさんの[　]（ほう）石（せき）をつけて(wear)パーティーに出（で）かけました。パーティーのホールには大（おお）きな水（すい）しょうの[　]（たま）(crystal ball) がありました。

31.　[　]（おう）復切符（ふくきっぷ）を買（か）うのですか？それではここにあなたとご[　]（しゅ）人（じん）の名前（なまえ）と[　]（じゅう）所（しょ）を書（か）いてください。

32.　ここは[　]（ちゅう）車場（しゃじょう）ではありません。[　]（ちゅう）意（い）してください。

33.　いろいろ仕（し）[　]（ごと）をさがして(seeking)、翻（ほん）[　]（やく）会社（がいしゃ）に[　]（き）まりました。[　]（えい）語（ご）の[　]（しょ）類（るい）を日本語（にほんご）に[　]（やく）しています。中（ちゅう）[　]（おう）線（せん）の[　]（かい）速電（そくでん）[　]（しゃ）で30分（ぷん）かかります(takes) が、朝(あさ)はたいへん混(こ)む(crowded)のでいつも[　](あし)をふまれます(trodden on)。[　](えき)から[　](ある)いて15分(ふん)ですが、おそく(late)なった時(とき)は、会社(かいしゃ)まで[　](はし)ります。

34. ハイキングのおべんとうは、すしのようなもの、[　](たと)えば海苔巻(のりまき)が一番好(いちばんす)きです。山道(やまみち)では一(いち)[　](れつ)になって[　](ある)かなければなりません。

35. わたしの会社(かいしゃ)ではダイヤモンドの指(ゆび)[　](わ)をベルギーから[　](ゆ)入(にゅう)して売(う)ります。大阪(おおさか)まで新(しん)[　](かん)線(せん)でよく出張(しゅっちょう)(business trip)します。

36. 大雪(おおゆき)のあとは、はやく[　](じょ)雪(せつ)しなければなりません。そして車(くるま)は[　](じょ)行(こう)のサインをまもります(obey)。

37. [　](しん)[　](がた)の特急電車(とっきゅうでんしゃ)は前(まえ)のほうの[　](かたち)が

とても美(うつく)しいカーブ(curved lines)になっています。

38. 二(に)[しゅう]間(かん)前(まえ)に両(りょう)[しん]といっしょに[あたら]しい家(いえ)にひっこしました(moved)。[きん][じょ]の[みち]や[とお]りの名前(なまえ)もおぼえました(memorized)。

39. うしろから、すごいスピードで車(くるま)が[せま]ってきてあっというまに(instantly)[お]い越(こ)して行(い)きました。わたしたちはこの町(まち)に[とま]るのですから、ゆっくり走(はし)りましょう。

40. 駅(えき)で定期(ていき)[けん]を買(か)います。それから本屋(ほんや)(bookstore)へ行(い)って源氏物語(げんじものがたり)(*The Tale of Genji*)の第二(だいに)[かん]を買(か)うつもりです。

41. 税金(ぜいきん)(tax)の[しん]告(こく)は3月(がつ)31日(にち)までです。今年(ことし)はたくさんはらわなければなりません。その理(り)[ゆう]は、家(いえ)の前(まえ)の[た]と[じん]社(じゃ)を右(みぎ)へ

[まが]ったところにある[ほそ]長(なが)い[はたけ]を売(う)ったからです。

42. [た]中(なか)さんは[じん]社(じゃ)のとなりにあるデパートの[しん]士服売場(しふくうりば)で働(はたら)いています。

43. あしたから、家(か)[ぞく]と[りょ]行(こう)します。

44. 「日本人(にほんじん)の[そ]先(せん)はどこから来(き)たか」というテレビの番(ばん)[ぐみ]を見(み)ました。

45. [ふく]都心(としん)に住(す)んでいる人々(ひとびと)は、公害(こうがい)(environmental pollution)のない幸(こう)[ふく]な生活(せいかつ)(life)をねがっています。

46. 警(けい)[さつ]のとなりにある神社(じんじゃ)の春(はる)[まつ]りは4月(がつ)15日(にち)です。

47. 学校(がっこう)の近(ちか)くに寺(てら)があります。教(きょう)[しつ]から本(ほん)[どう]の美(うつく)しい[や]根(ね)が見(み)えます。本(ほん)[や]や小(ちい)さな[　](みせ)もあります。

48. 「どんな[　](いえ)が地震(じしん)に[　](あん)心(しん)できるか」というテーマで研(けん)[　](きゅう)レポートを書(か)いています。[　](から)手(て)のけいこのあとで先生(せんせい)のお[　](たく)へよって(drop by)、本(ほん)をかりて(borrow)くるつもりです。

49. 明治神(めいじじん)[　](ぐう)(Meiji Shrine)の近(ちか)くに外交(がいこう)[　](かん)のアパートがあって、受付(うけつ)けには[　](かん)理人(りにん)がいます。

50. 骨(こつ)とう[　](いち)できれいな[　](ぬの)と財(さい)[　](ふ)を買(か)いました。

51. 東京(とうきょう)は大(おお)きな首(しゅ)[　](と)ですから東京(とうきょう)[　](と)といいます。アメリカの州(しゅう)(state)にあたる(equivalent)のは、日本(にほん)では県(けん)です。県(けん)の中(なか)には大(おお)きな[　](し)もありますが、大(だい)[　](ぶ)分(ぶん)は小(ちい)さい村(むら)

(villages)です。村があつまった(grouped together)ものを[　　]といいます。たとえば、住所は、[　　]馬県山田[　　]東村というようにいいます。

52. 今[　　]の日曜日、石の[　　]がある寺の[　　]禅会に出[　　]するつもりです。

53. 日本は資[　　]のない国ですが、美しい高[　　]は多いのです。

54. かぜをひいたので、病院の内[　　]でみてもらってから、[　　]金をはらいました。

55. もうすぐ[　　]人が40％になる社会を[　　]えなければなりません。

56. うちの会社とA社の関[　　]ですか？同じ[　　]列の会社なんですよ。A社は製[　　]業をやっていますがね。

57. これから100mのレースがはじまります。グラウンド(sports ground)の白(しろ)い[　(せん)　]の前(まえ)に選手(せんしゅ)たち(athletes)がならんでいます。いい記(き)[　(ろく)　]が出(で)るとうれしいですね。スタジアムのまわりに見(み)える木(き)の[　(みどり)　]が美(うつく)しいです。

58. 現代(げんだい)(nowadays)に電(でん)[　(わ)　]のない生(せい)[　(かつ)　]は考(かんが)えられません。

59. オリンピックが[　(はじ)　]まると、政(せい)[　(じ)　]のニュースよりもスポーツの記事(きじ)(articles)がよく[　(よ)　]まれます。ゲームは二週間(にしゅうかん)ぐらい[　(つづ)　]きます。

60. 年寄(としよ)り(elderly people)がふえていくので、いろいろ[　(せつ)　]備(び)をするために、消費(しょうひ)[　(ぜい)　]を高(たか)くしなければならないと、政府(せいふ)は[　(せつ)　]明(めい)しています。

61. おなかが、痛(いた)くて[　(くる)　]しいので、[　(くすり)　]屋(や)で[　(くすり)　]を買(か)ってきてのむつもりです。少(すこ)し[　(らく)　]

になったら、[　わか　]い人たちの音（おん）[　がく　]を聴（き）いて[　たの　]しもうと思（おも）います。

62.　小学（しょうがっ）[　こう　]の生徒（せいと）は漢字（かんじ）のホームワークを毎日一（まいにちいち）[　まい　]書（か）かなければなりません。

63.　この[　むら　]は[　りん　]業（ぎょう）がさかん(thriving)で、よい木（もく）[　ざい　]ができます。

64.　この[　はやし　]には[　まつ　]と[　すぎ　]の木（き）があります。[　えだ　]ぶりのよい[　まつ　]が見（み）えますよ。ほとんど枯（か）れ(withered)そうになった木（き）を元気（げんき）にさせる[　ぎ　]術（じゅつ）はすごいですね。

65.　図書館（としょかん）(library)が[　あ　]くとすぐ入って、[　へい　]館（かん）するまで何時（なんじ）[　かん　]も本（ほん）を読（よ）んだり、調（しら）べたりしています(researching)。学（がく）[　もん　]を続（つづ）けることは[　つよ　]い気持（きも）ちがいるし、体（からだ）が

[よわ]かったらできません。

66. 政府(せいふ)は今年(ことし)の[けい]画(かく)と[ほう]針(しん)を出(だ)しました。

67. わたしの家(いえ)は駅(えき)の近(ちか)くです。お[か]子屋(しや)と[くだ]物屋(ものや)の[あいだ]ですよ。古(ふる)い(old)家(いえ)ですから、入口(いりぐち)に鳥(とり)の[す]が見(み)えますよ。簡(かん)[たん]な地図(ちず)を書(か)きましょうか。

68. わたしが[く]らしている近所(きんじょ)の[ぼ]地(ち)には、江戸(えど)[ばく]府(ふ)の将軍(しょうぐん)の[はか]があります。

69. 大学(だいがく)で「経済(けいざい)(economics)の[こう]造(ぞう)」という[こう]義(ぎ)をきいています。

70. 病院(びょういん)の[かん]護婦(ごふ)はたいてい白(しろ)いユニホームを[き]ています。

71. 村(むら)[ざと]ばかりでなく、大都市(だいとし)の中(なか)にまっ[くろ]なからす(crow)が食(た)べ物(もの)をさがして飛(と)んできます。

72. 日本(にほん)で水産業(すいさんぎょう)(fisheries)は[　](じゅう)要(よう)な(important)産業(さんぎょう)(industry)でしたが、今(いま)ではとれる[　](さかな)の[　](りょう)が少(すく)なくなりました。

73. 秋(あき)[　](ば)れの日曜日(にちようび)、[　](せい)流(りゅう)のそばを歩(ある)いていると、[　](せい)神(しん)まで[　](きよ)められる気(き)がします。それに、いなかには人(にん)[　](じょう)(human nature)のあたたかさがあります。

74. このごろは、[　](あか)るいニュースよりも心(こころ)が[　](くら)くなるニュースのほうが多(おお)いです。

75. 毎(まい)[　](ばん)よく[　](べん)強(きょう)します。

76. [　](げん)実(じつ)(reality)は[　](り)想(そう)(ideals)どおりにはいきません。

77. 秋(あき)の学(がっ)[　](き)はじめに満(まん)[　](ちょう)と干(かん)[　](ちょう)の

時間(じかん)を調(しら)べたレポートを出(だ)さなければなりません。今(いま)は夏休(なつやす)みで山中(やまなか)[こ]にいますが、[あさ]と[ばん]はすずしいので[べん]強(きょう)しています。

78. 北海道(ほっかいどう)にいる友(とも)だちの[でん]話(わ)では、もう[ゆき]がふったそうです。今日(きょう)の東京(とうきょう)は[くも]りです。空(そら)にはあつい(thick)[くも]が見(み)えるので、夕方(ゆうがた)は[らい]雨(う)になるかもしれません。

79. 御(ご)[はん]はよくかんで(chew)食(た)べます。[さけ]は少(すこ)ししか[の]みませんから、病気(びょうき)の心(しん)[ぱい]はありません。

80. 食事(しょくじ)のあとで、すぐ[さら]をあらいます。[けつ]圧(あつ)がさがるように薬(くすり)も[の]みます。

81. [あつ]い季節(きせつ)になると、悪(わる)いことをする[もの]がふえるので、警察(けいさつ)[しょ]は忙(いそが)しいです。

82. [　　](しゅう)入(にゅう)のある人(ひと)はすべて税金(ぜいきん)を[　　](と)られます。

83. 総理大臣(そうりだいじん)(Prime Minister)の田中(たなか)[　　](し)は、国(こく)[　　](みん)に政府(せいふ)の考(かんが)えを話(はな)しました。

84. よく[　　](ねむ)れなくて目(め)が赤(あか)くなったので病院(びょういん)(hospital)の[　　](がん)科(か)でみてもらいました。

85. バルコニーに[　　](しょく)物(ぶつ)を[　　](お)きました。産地(さんち)[　　](ちょく)売(ばい)(direct from the producing center)ですから、[　　](ね)段(だん)も安(やす)かったです。

86. 京都(きょうと)の古(ふる)い寺(てら)の周(しゅう)[　　](い)は地(ち)[　　](ず)を持(も)った[　　](だん)体旅行(たいりょこう)の人(ひと)たちでいつも混(こ)んでいます。

87. 急(きゅう)に車(くるま)がパンク(puncture)して[　　](こま)りました。ガソリンスタンドの人(ひと)の説明(せつめい)で原(げん)[　　](いん)がわかりました。

88. 親(おや)は子(こ)どもを育(そだ)てる時(とき)、休(きゅう)[　](そく)する時間(じかん)がないほど[　](いそが)しいのです。いつも子(こ)どものことを[　](おも)っています。その親(おや)の[　](おん)を[　](わす)れてはいけません。

89. 女(じょ)[　](せい)が結婚(けっこん)すると、ふつう主人(しゅじん)の方(ほう)の[　](せい)に変(か)わります。

90. 子(こ)どもたちは親(おや)の大(おお)きな[　](あい)を[　](う)けて成長(せいちょう)しています(growing up)。[　](か)わらないのが[　](あい)だと[　](おも)いますが、[　](こい)は[　](か)わりやすいものだと[　](おも)いませんか。

91. [　](わたくし)と[　](いもうと)は戦争中(せんそうちゅう)(during the war)に結(けっ)[　](こん)しました。農家(のうか)(farming family)の[　](よめ)になった[　](わたくし)たちは家族(かぞく)みんなで[　](かせ)がなければなりませんでした。平(へい)[　](わ)になってから生(う)まれた[　](むすめ)は、結(けっ)[　](こん)よりも社会(しゃかい)(society)で働(はたら)くことに興(きょう)[　　](み)があります。

92.　子(こ)どもたちが学校(がっこう)から[　　](かえ)るまでの間(あいだ)、パート(part-time)で働(はたら)いている主(しゅ)[　　](ふ)がふえました。

93.　あたたかな[　　](き)節(せつ)になったので、ハイキングに出(で)かけます。クラスの[　　](い)員(いん)は行(い)きたい人(ひと)は何人(なんにん)か、しらべてください。

94.　大(おお)[　　](さか)[　　](じょう)まで、[　　](さか)道(みち)をのぼって行(い)かなければなりません。むかし、[　　](しろ)のまわりの地(ち)[　　](いき)には、さむらいたちが住(す)んでいました。あの橋(はし)も[　　](いた)でつくってありましたよ。

95.　ごちそうをいただいて満(まん)[　　](ぷく)です。エネルギーが出(で)ましたから、今晩(こんばん)は[　　](ふく)雑(ざつ)な文法(ぶんぽう)(grammar)の[　　](ふく)習(しゅう)をがんばりましょう。

96. 私(わたくし)は胃(い)[　](ちょう)が弱(よわ)いので、太(たい)[　](よう)の当(あ)たる(exposed to the sun)[　](ば)所(しょ)で、かるい運動(うんどう)をしてから少(すこ)しぬるい(lukewarm)お[　](ゆ)のお風呂(ふろ)に毎日(まいにち)入(はい)っています。

97. この商店(しょうてん)[　](がい)を出(で)たところに美(び)[　](じゅつ)館(かん)があります。

98. 天皇(てんのう)[　](へい)下(か)はヨーロッパ大(たい)[　](りく)の訪問(ほうもん)(visit)からお帰(かえ)りになり空港(くうこう)(airport)につきました。まもなくここの[　](かい)段(だん)をおりていらっしゃいます。

99. 海(かい)[　](がん)(coast)の[　](すな)浜(はま)(sand beach)を歩(ある)いていると、20[　](びょう)ごと(every)に大(おお)きな波(なみ)(wave)がよってきて(approaches)、海(うみ)の中(なか)の[　](いわ)がかくれてしまいます(disappears)。

100. ひっこしした(moved to a new address)

友(とも)だちから、まだ手紙(てがみ)の[へん]事(じ)が来(こ)ないのです。きょ年(ねん)この[へん]に住(す)んでいた友(とも)だちなんですがね。

101. 子(こ)どもを[つ]れて毎日(まいにち)[うん]動(どう)します。

102. 国(くに)の工業(こうぎょう)(industry)は[しん]歩(ぽ)発(はっ)[たつ]しました。

103. [そく][たつ]で郵(ゆう)[そう]しましたから[おそ]くても明日(あした)の午後(ごご)に着(つ)くはずです。

104. 会社(かいしゃ)を[たい]職(しょく)してから、いなかで生活(せいかつ)をはじめました。大(だい)[こん](radish)の植(う)えてある道(みち)を、制(せい)[げん]スピード35kmでゆっくり運転(うんてん)して町(まち)へ行(い)きます。

105. 彼(かれ)は俳優(はいゆう)(actor)です。こんどの映画(えいが)で階(かい)[だん]から悪者(わるもの)を[な]げて[ころ]す[やく](role)をもらいました。

106. 三年前、友だちのパーティーに[　]待された時に、今の家内(wife)を[　]介されました。

107. ビザの[　]長ができたのでこれからも[　]康に気をつけながら、[　]築の勉強にがんばります。

108. 戦国時代(the Warring States period)の大名(daimyo)は[　]に家族を人質(hostage)として送りました。それが自分の領土(territory)をまもる(protect)ための[　]当なやりかた(way of doing)でした。

109. むずかしい問[　]で社長は[　]を使うので[　]の色もわるいです。会社の経済がよくなるように[　]っています。

110. アルバイトでもらったお金を銀行で

[　]金しました。それから本を買いに行きました。本屋では[　]収書をもらいました。

111. パンダ(panda)には二種[　]ありますが、私たちが見ているのはジャイアントパンダです。だんだん[　]が少なくなっていくのは、ざんねんです。

112. 少し[　]本ができたら、山中百[　]店の前に[　]自転車屋を開きたいのです。家[　]と自転車を買う[　]用ぐらいあればいいでしょう。ほんとうは品[　]のよい電気製品を輸出する[　]易会社をつくりたいのですが、[　]乏な私にはとてもむりです。

113. 外国旅行では[　]重品に気をつけてください。お金をへやにおいて、なくなってもホテルは[　]任をとって(take responsibility)

くれません。トラベラーズチェック(traveler's checks)を持って行くことに[さん]成です。両[がえ]する時は銀行(bank)がいいと思います。

114. 山のように本を[つ]み上げて読んでいます。よいレポートを書いて学校の成[せき]をよくしたいと思いますから。

115. 日本では車は道の左[がわ]を走るのが規[そく]です。外国から来た人は車の大きさや道の幅(width)を[はか]るのが, なれる(become accustomed)まではむずかしいでしょうか。

116. 大[ぜい]の学生たちは英語の[じゅく]語を[ねっ]心におぼえています(learning)。

117. 大[ぶつ]が見たい時、寺の入口で300円ほど[はら]わなければなりません。

118. [　　]服(uniform)の生地(cloth)は中国[　　]です。

119. 運転免許証(driver's license)を取るためにむずかしい試[　　]を受けなければなりません。また、古い車で走るのは危[　　]なので、車[　　]の制度があります。

120. [　　]場(workplace)という組[　　]では、経[　　]といつも新しい知[　　]が求められます(is required)。

ANSWER KEY

1. (日) (目) (日) (白) (百)
2. (自) (首)
3. (売) (貝) (見) (買) (員)
4. (天) (太) (大) (犬) (少) (小) (犬) (犬) (元)
5. (右) (方) (上) (万) (上) (左) (方) (万) (下)
6. (右) (少) (左) (方) (力) (刀)
7. (休) (九) (体) (体) (人) (入) (丸)
8. (使) (方) (便)
9. (昨) (作) (手) (予) (便) (手) (子) (毛) (毛) (便) (右) (左)
10. (学) (学) (字)
11. (動) (働)
12. (特) (待) (物) (時) (持)
13. (土) (士)
14. (社) (仕)
15. (母) (毎) (海) (梅)
16. (友) (池) (東) (交) (他) (友) (反) (西) (交) (父) (交) (文) (地) (束)
17. (四) (花) (雨) (両) (花)
18. (先) (生) (光) (光) (冊) (四) (用) (円)
19. (北) (東) (化) (西) (化) (両) (化) (比)
20. (会) (各) (名)
21. (会) (金) (金) (全) (合)
22. (旬) (句)
23. (牛) (羊) (半) (来) (来) (午) (午) (平) (美) (末) (未)
24. (矢) (失)
25. (水) (氷) (水) (永)
26. (島) (鳥) (島) (馬)
27. (河) (可)
28. (何) (同) (向) (符) (荷)
29. (府) (付)
30. (王) (宝) (玉)
31. (往) (主) (住)

32. （駐）（注）
33. （事）（訳）（決）（英）
（書）（訳）（央）（快）
（車）（足）（駅）（歩）
（走）
34. （例）（列）（歩）
35. （輪）（輸）（幹）
36. （除）（徐）
37. （新）（型）（形）
38. （週）（親）（新）（近）
（所）（道）（通）
39. （迫）（追）（泊）
40. （券）（巻）
41. （申）（由）（田）（神）
（曲）（細）（畑）
42. （田）（神）（紳）
43. （族）（旅）
44. （祖）（組）
45. （副）（福）
46. （察）（祭）
47. （室）（堂）（屋）（屋）
（店）
48. （家）（安）（究）（空）
（宅）
49. （宮）（官）（管）
50. （市）（布）（布）
51. （都）（都）（市）（部）
（郡）（群）（郡）
52. （度）（庭）（座）（席）
53. （源）（原）
54. （科）（料）
55. （老）（考）
56. （係）（系）（糸）
57. （線）（録）（緑）
58. （話）（活）
59. （始）（治）（読）（続）
60. （設）（税）（説）
61. （苦）（薬）（薬）（楽）
（若）（楽）（楽）
62. （校）（枚）
63. （村）（林）（材）
64. （林）（松）（杉）（枝）
（松）（技）
65. （開）（閉）（間）（問）
（強）（弱）
66. （計）（方）
67. （菓）（果）（間）（巣）
（単）
68. （暮）（墓）（幕）（墓）
69. （構）（講）
70. （看）（着）
71. （里）（黒）
72. （重）（魚）（量）
73. （晴）（清）（精）（清）
（情）
74. （明）（暗）

75. (晩) (勉)
76. (現) (理)
77. (期) (潮) (潮) (湖)
(朝) (晩) (勉)
78. (電) (雪) (曇) (雲)
(雷)
79. (飯) (酒) (飲) (配)
80. (皿) (血) (飲)
81. (暑) (者) (署)
82. (収) (取)
83. (氏) (民)
84. (眠) (眼)
85. (植) (置) (直) (値)
86. (囲) (図) (団)
87. (困) (因)
88. (息) (忙) (思) (恩)
(忘)
89. (性) (姓)
90. (愛) (受) (変) (愛)
(思) (恋) (変) (思)
91. (私) (妹) (婚) (嫁)
(私) (稼) (和) (娘)
(婚) (味)
92. (帰) (婦)
93. (季) (委)
94. (阪) (城) (坂) (城)
(域) (板)
95. (腹) (複) (復)
96. (腸) (陽) (場) (湯)
97. (街) (術)
98. (陛) (陸) (階)
99. (岸) (砂) (秒) (岩)
100. (返) (辺)
101. (連) (運)
102. (進) (達)
103. (速) (達) (送) (遅)
104. (退) (根) (限)
105. (段) (投) (殺) (役)
106. (招) (紹)
107. (延) (健) (建)
108. (敵) (適)
109. (題) (頭) (顔) (願)
110. (預) (領)
111. (類) (数)
112. (資) (貨) (貸) (賃)
(費) (質) (貿) (貧)
113. (貴) (責) (賛) (替)
114. (積) (績)
115. (側) (則) (測)
116. (勢) (熟) (熱)
117. (仏) (払)
118. (制) (製)
119. (験) (険) (検)
120. (職) (織) (験) (識)

ABOUT THE AUTHOR

Tae Moriyama graduated from the Faculty of Literature of Waseda University, and has been teaching the Japanese language to foreigners for more than 30 years. In 1973 she established the Modern Japanese Language School in Tokyo, where she continues to serve as director. She has taught people from more than 30 countries and from all walks of life, including journalists, lawyers, English language instructors, business executives, translators and specialists in Japanese culture and history. This experience has given her a deep understanding as to which aspects of Japanese are the most difficult for foreigners to master.

In addition to a series of textbooks for Japanese language education, Tae Moriyama has previously published four books. These are The Practical Guide to Japanese Signs Parts I and II (Kodansha International, 1986), compiled from a series of columns entitled "Signs Will Tell You" that appeared in the Mainichi Daily News over a period of several years, and two historical travel guides published by Shufunotomo, Weekend Adventures Outside Tokyo (1990) and Tokyo Adventures (1993).

Plans are in hand for a third book in the historical travel guide series, which the author is currently researching.

201	糸	221	枚	241	墓	261	現	281	取
202	系	222	林	242	暮	262	理	282	収
203	係	223	村	243	幕	263	朝	283	氏
204	線	224	材	244	構	264	期	284	民
205	緑	225	松	245	講	265	湖	285	眼
206	録	226	杉	246	着	266	潮	286	眠
207	話	227	枝	247	看	267	電	287	直
208	活	228	技	248	里	268	雪	288	置
209	治	229	問	249	黒	269	雷	289	植
210	始	230	間	250	魚	270	雲	290	値
211	読	231	開	251	重	271	曇	291	囲
212	続	232	閉	252	量	272	酒	292	図
213	説	233	強	253	晴	273	配	293	団
214	設	234	弱	254	清	274	飯	294	困
215	税	235	計	255	精	275	飲	295	因
216	楽	236	針	256	情	276	皿	296	恩
217	薬	237	果	257	明	277	血	297	思
218	若	238	菓	258	暗	278	者	298	息
219	苦	239	巣	259	晩	279	暑	299	忘
220	校	240	単	260	勉	280	署	300	忙

301	性	321	板	341	辺	361	適	381	貴
302	姓	322	城	342	連	362	敵	382	責
303	受	323	域	343	運	363	顔	383	積
304	愛	324	腹	344	達	364	頭	384	績
305	恋	325	複	345	進	365	願	385	則
306	変	326	復	346	送	366	題	386	測
307	私	327	場	347	速	367	預	387	側
308	和	328	湯	348	遅	368	領	388	熱
309	味	329	陽	349	退	369	類	389	勢
310	妹	330	腸	350	根	370	数	390	熟
311	娘	331	街	351	限	371	貸	391	払
312	婚	332	術	352	投	372	貿	392	仏
313	嫁	333	階	353	殺	373	貧	393	制
314	稼	334	陛	354	役	374	貨	394	製
315	帰	335	陸	355	段	375	賃	395	験
316	婦	336	岸	356	招	376	資	396	検
317	季	337	岩	357	紹	377	質	397	険
318	委	338	砂	358	建	378	費	398	識
319	坂	339	秒	359	延	379	賛	399	織
320	阪	340	返	360	健	380	替	400	職